# TCP/IP AND NFS™

## Internetworking in a UNIX™ Environment

# TCP/IP AND NFS™

## Internetworking in a UNIX™ Environment

## Michael Santifaller

Santix software gmbh

Translated by Stephen S. Wilson

ADDISON-WESLEY
PUBLISHING
COMPANY

Wokingham, England · Reading, Massachusetts · Menlo Park, California · New York
Don Mills, Ontario · Amsterdam · Bonn · Sydney · Singapore
Tokyo · Madrid · San Juan · Milan · Paris · Mexico City · Seoul · Taipei

Cover designed by Chris Eley and
printed by The Riverside Printing Co. (Reading) Ltd.
Printed in Great Britain by Mackays of Chatham plc, Chatham, Kent.

First printed 1991. Reprinted 1991 (twice) and 1992.

**British Library Cataloguing in Publication Data**
Santifaller, Michael
    TCP/IP and NFS internetworking in a UNIX environment.
    1. Computers. Networks
    I. Title   II. [TCP/IP und NFS in Theorie und Praxis].
    *English*
    004.6

    ISBN 0-201-54432-6

**Library of Congress Cataloging-in-Publication Data**
Santifaller, Michael.
    [TCP/IP und NFS in Theorie und Praxis. English]
    TCP/IP and NFS : internetworking in a UNIX environment / Michael
Santifaller ; translated by Stephen S. Wilson.
        p.   cm.
    Translation of: TCP/IP und NFS in Theorie und Praxis.
    Includes bibliographical references and index.
    ISBN 0-201-54432-6
    1. Local area networks (Computer networks)   2. UNIX (Computer
operating system)   I. Title.
TK5105.7.S27   1991
004.6'8--dc20                                           90-26268
                                                           CIP

# Preface

I first heard about NFS in 1984 when I began working with 4.2BSD and TCP/IP. At the same time, I was a witness to the intensive OSI discussions which were then under way. In common with many other UNIX developers who, like myself, were convinced from year to year that the next year would bring the breakthrough for UNIX, I then believed that, after a brief blossoming, TCP/IP and NFS would generally be replaced by the corresponding protocols from the ISO world.

Thus, I am even more surprised today to find that interest in these three technologies by the commercial data-processing world is in fact only now appearing. While this is very regrettable (in fact, it has often caused me great frustration over recent years), I am today convinced that the age of PCs and of MS-DOS was important and necessary. Through their experiences with the PC, users have learnt to apply the computer as a tool, and to understand the software which runs on it, despite its partial inadequacy. In addition, the user is today also willing to accept a system with the complexity of UNIX, since he must perceive that performance exacts its price, as can be seen from the example of OS/2 with its storage requirements and its use of processor cycles. On the other hand, in recent years, the ranks of UNIX gurus have been augmented by people for whom the operation of a computer is merely a means to an end and not the substance of life, and this has greatly improved the reputation of the UNIX operating system.

Another major change has also taken place in recent years. With the introduction of PCs on users' desks, users have come of age and hardware and software suppliers can no longer palm off products which have no apparent advantage other than their architectural conformity. *De facto* standards are accorded the importance they deserve. Manufacturers have, on the other hand, learnt that open, non-proprietary systems in which components, data and above all the knowledge about software and hardware are themselves portable and interchangeable, and bring advantages for all sides. Our three technologies are examples of these principles:

- UNIX for portability to different hardware platforms.
- TCP/IP for reliable exchange of data between heterogeneous systems.
- NFS for transparent integration of heterogeneous computer systems into the network.

If we consider the history of UNIX, TCP/IP and NFS, it is conspicuous that, measured by the rapid pace of the data-processing industry, all three technologies are relatively old soldiers and, in the case of UNIX and TCP/IP, even real veterans. This could lead one to conclude that other technologies, presently being developed or standardized, may have to wait some time before their breakthrough occurs.

It may be that all good things take time to mature. For you, the reader, this will mean that, after reading this book, you will be able to use (exploit) your newly acquired knowledge for quite some time. Have fun!

## Acknowledgements

At this point I would like to thank several people who have supported me during the production of this book:

Hans Strack-Zimmermann, who led me from the back benches to the front line and thus made everything possible in the first place.

Stefan Vogel, who was a great help as a technical conscience and a discussion partner during the correction of the manuscript.

My colleagues at iXOS, without whose tolerance nothing would have worked out.

And, in particular, my wife Frau Christa and my two sons, Christoph and Marvin, who left me in peace, when necessary.

In addition, I heartily thank the Addison-Wesley Publishing Company for its commendable co-operation during the publication of this book.

*Michael Santifaller*
January 1991

For reasons of simplicity, the pronoun 'he' is used to relate to both male and female throughout the book.

# Contents

## Trademark notice

386/ix$^{TM}$ is a trademark of Interactive Systems Incorporated.
DCE$^{TM}$ and OSF/1$^{TM}$ are trademarks of Open Software Foundation.
DYNIX$^{TM}$ is a trademark of Sequent Computer Systems Incorporated.
Ethernet$^{TM}$ and XNS$^{TM}$ are trademarks of Xerox Corporation.
iXOS$^{TM}$ is a trademark of iXOS Software GmbH.
Macintosh$^{TM}$ and LocalTalk$^{TM}$ are trademarks of Apple Corporation.
MS-DOS$^{TM}$, MS-OS/2$^{TM}$, LAN Manager/X$^{TM}$ and XENIX$^{TM}$ are trademarks of
        MicroSoft Corporation.
NFS$^{TM}$, NIS$^{TM}$, SPARC$^{TM}$ and SunOS$^{TM}$ are trademarks of Sun Microsystems
        Incorporated.
SINIX$^{TM}$ is a trademark of Siemens AG.
UNIX$^{TM}$, RFS$^{TM}$ and System V$^{TM}$ are trademarks of AT&T.
VAX$^{TM}$, VMS$^{TM}$, DEC station$^{TM}$ and Ultrix$^{TM}$ are trademarks of Digital Equipment
        Corporation.

# Introduction

## About this book

This book was developed from course material prepared on the same topic for iXOS Software GmbH. The book is not intended for specialists only. However, anyone who wishes to know even more details of the individual protocols described here or of specific algorithms is referred to the sources listed in the Bibliography. Nor is the book intended as a reference or a replacement for a manual. Whether you are a user, an administrator or a developer, the book should ease your entry into the world of UNIX systems networked with TCP/IP and NFS. It may possibly give you an appetite for networks and it should help you to tackle acute problems.

As far as the choice of topics is concerned, the characteristics of TCP/IP and NFS architectures mean that their protocols appear in various forms and guises on a large variety of computer systems. Every run-time environment has individual features which influence user and programmer interfaces, as well as the nature of available networking options.

A presentation and discussion of this variety would occupy all the space in this book several times over. Thus, we shall restrict ourselves to the operation of TCP/IP and NFS on computers running under the UNIX operating system, and within this topic to those areas which give an understanding of the architecture, of the interfaces and of their uses. Even on UNIX systems there are many differences in comprehensiveness and functionality.

This book is not a guide to the implementation of any of the protocols described, rather the intention is to enable you to understand what is happening in the computer and in the transmission medium when you use a command or programmer interface. This understanding will also help you to diagnose errors more rapidly and to correct any problems.

Some of the themes of this book can only be touched on; thus, the following areas are at best discussed in brief:

- gateway protocols
- routing
- network management
- domain name service, name server and resolver
- electronic mail.

Experience shows that most UNIX networks currently used in industry are too small to justify the installation of network management and routing. Electronic mail, and in particular the UNIX program *sendmail*, would fill a book on its own. The reader is referred to the literature available in the product documentation, which is usually sufficiently comprehensive to support the work of the system administrator.

## Description of the notation used

As is generally the custom, different typefaces have been used to facilitate understanding and for emphasis:

- New terms are introduced in *italics*. Terms shown in this way are listed in either the Glossary or the Index.
- A `typewriter font` is used for screen output and program listings.
- All user entries in screen dialogues together with program and path names are given in an *`italic typewriter font`*.

## Standards

Many readers will immediately ask themselves how they should rate the information from the following pages. Thus, to clarify the situation right from the start, here are a few comments on standards.

Only one of the protocols described in this book is a world-wide standard in the sense of an official norm from ISO, IEEE, DIN or other body; namely, the IEEE 802.3 standard for local area network technology. However, this does not imply that no reference specifications exist for all other protocols in the TCP/IP and NFS world and that implementations are at the discretion of individual manufacturers.

As you will find out in the following chapters, most protocols of the TCP/IP architecture are specified by a so-called *RFC* (Request For Comment). RFCs are publications for the Internet community; namely, those people and institutions who belong to the ARPA-Internet (more about the ARPA-Internet in Chapter 2). RFCs are published by the IAB (Internet Activities Board). They may be obtained either by electronic mail from the *Network Information Centre* (NIC) at the *Stanford Research Institute* (SRI) or in machine-readable form by file transfer from a computer in the NIC. The precise addresses for information about RFCs are given in an appendix.

Both specifications of individual protocols and articles about general problems of network operation are published in the RFCs. Not all the protocols published in RFCs are at the same time also Internet standards. A standard is first declared after verification by the IAB and a six-month transition period (draft standard). In total, approximately 1200 RFCs have now been issued. Relevant RFCs are listed in the Bibliography, and the RFC numbers are given in the discussions of the individual protocols.

Since uniform standards are in the interest of both the user and the manufacturer, the RFC specifications are overwhelmingly adhered to in all TCP/IP and NFS implementations known to the author. Compatibility is increased by the fact that the products of most manufacturers are based on the same source code and are additionally tested against generally recognized reference machines (for example, the Sun workstation for NFS). However, there are some differences in the robustness of the implementations (that is, system failures occur or connections are left hanging).

In addition to being Internet standards, IP, ICMP, TCP, FTP and SMTP have also been declared to be *MIL-STD* (the standard of the US military). These standards are laid down in publications of the *Department of Defence* (DOD). Although RFC and MIL-STD specifications are formulated in very different ways, the protocols they specify are largely identical.

In addition to the official and semi-official standards, there are also the much valued industry standards, developed by copying the interfaces and functions of the product of a market-leading competitor, which cannot be the worst for the user. This category includes the NFS protocols and the well-known Berkeley utilities, with which we shall become acquainted later.

When talking about standards, we should not omit to mention the validation of implementations in respect of conformance with the standard. Like many other things, this point is handled pragmatically in the TCP/IP and NFS worlds. There are at present no official test specifications for TCP/IP. As previously mentioned, individual implementations are tested against a generally complete and seemingly robust implementation from another manufacturer. For NFS, a package of test programs is available for the licensee of the reference implementation source code, which may be used to test various aspects of the operation of NFS. But this proof can scarcely be termed validation. An annual meeting (so-called *connectathon*) in California is organized on this topic by Sun Microsystems, at which manufacturers can test their NFS implementations against each other. This means that problems with the implementation of NFS or with the underlying protocols are as a rule soon recognized. Other test venues include the so-called *multivendor shows* at computer fairs, when, even here in Europe, computers from different manufacturers intercommunicate on a single network for demonstration purposes. If you are looking for a form of seal of approval for UNIX networking, you will be disappointed, since there is no such thing at present.

# 1

# Protocols

- Why do we need protocols?
- The Open Systems Interconnection reference model
- Tasks of a protocol
- Connection-oriented and connectionless protocols

In this book, we shall talk a great deal about protocols. Therefore, before we begin the discussion of TCP/IP and NFS, it is sensible to reiterate briefly certain fundamental things about protocols.

## Why do we need protocols?

Computer applications communicate with one another by so-called *protocols*. Protocols are rules which co-ordinate the exchange of messages between partners and thus make this exchange efficient, much as a certain formalism is required for understanding between people. An example of a protocol in the human world is the use of 'Roger' and 'Over' in radio traffic: both communication partners acknowledge that they have understood the message with 'Roger' and signal a change in the direction of speech with 'Over'.

Data exchange between data-processing systems naturally involves similar but also more extensive requirements, as we shall see in the next section. Because of the complexity of communication between data-processing systems, it is not sensible to execute all the necessary tasks in a single protocol. Thus, it is usual to apply several data-communication protocols simultaneously, which, in the form of several overlaid protocol layers with different functions, co-operate and together provide a service for the user.

## The Open Systems Interconnection reference model

In order to provide a uniform way of viewing the functions to be executed at each level, the *International Standardization Organization* (ISO) has proposed a protocol-layering model ('architecture model'), the so-called *Open Systems Interconnection* (OSI) seven-layer reference model (OSI, 1984).

This model, shown in Figure 1.1, is at present generally used as a framework in which to describe protocol characteristics and functions. In addition, it forms the basis for the development and standardization of ISO's own standard protocol layers. As a rule, every collection of protocols (including TCP/IP) has its own architecture, whose layers incorporate the individual protocols and their functions. Although in the following pages we discuss the TCP/IP architecture model in detail, we still use the ISO nomenclature, since this is generally known and recognized.

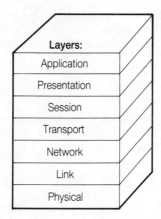

**Figure 1.1**   OSI reference model.

The layering is based on the principle that any layer (for example, the network layer) may use the services of the layer below it (in this case the link layer) without knowing how the latter provides these services. The layer above (in this case the transport layer) is offered a specific service of its own. The effect of this is to distribute the work across the layers. The major tasks of the protocol layers in the OSI model, as far as our consideration of the TCP/IP architecture is concerned, may be defined as follows.

## Physical layer

This controls, among other things, the exchange of individual information bits (relating to transmission rate, bit coding, connection, etc.) over a transmission medium. Usually, the function of this layer is closely related to that of the overlying link layer. *X.21* and *RS232*, among other things, also specify characteristics of the physical layer.

## Link layer

The task of this layer is to ensure the reliable transmission of information units (packets or blocks) and to address stations connected to the transmission medium. *HDLC* and *CSMA/CD* are examples of protocols here (see Chapter 3).

### Network layer

The main task of this layer is to establish virtual paths between stations in the network, for example, by transmitting packets via switching nodes. IP is resident in this layer. Another well-known protocol is *X.25*.

### Transport layer

This layer is responsible for transporting messages between communication partners; it usually controls the data flow and ensures that the data is not corrupted. TCP and UDP are transport protocols (see Chapter 3).

### Session layer

This layer controls the exchange of messages in the transport connection (for example, change of transfer direction, session restart after interruption of a connection, etc.). One very well-known protocol of this class is *LU6.2*. In the chapter on NFS protocols (Chapter 9), we shall also consider the RPC protocol in more detail.

### Presentation layer

Computer systems sometimes use different methods of encoding text, numbers, etc. In this layer, it is determined how data types are to be encoded so that they may be exchanged between different systems. Examples here are *ASN.1* and *XDR*.

### Application layer

The protocols which run in the application layer are defined by the task-specific programs (for example, for file transfer, database queries, etc.).

## Tasks of a protocol

In addition to the addressing of the communication end points, the control of data flow and many other things, one of the main tasks of protocols is usually to provide reliable data-transmission services. Table 1.1 lists some of the most important tasks of protocols and examples of how they are implemented.

**Table 1.1**  Tasks of protocols.

| Task | How implemented |
|------|-----------------|
| Error detection | Checksums, sequence numbers, acknowledgements, watchdog timers |
| Error elimination | Retransmission of packets, correction methods (for example, *Hamming codes*) |
| Addressing | Address fields |
| Flow control | Receive windows, acknowledgements |

Networks, computers and data lines are in no way reliable against the corruption of transmitted data or against a system failure. Since a user of a network service, whether an end-user at a terminal or a protocol in a higher-ranking layer, expects error-free data, data-transmission problems must be first identified and then, if possible, resolved.

Data corruption during transmission, together with data loss, are among the most frequent problems. In large networks, a message may also be jumbled, for example, when a node sends the individual component packets of a message over several paths in the network. Here, we must ensure that the data is forwarded to the destination in the same order in which it was sent by the source (*sequencing*). Another common problem in data communication is that, usually, the sender sends the data more rapidly than the recipient is able to accept it and process it further. In order to prevent loss of data, the sender must, if necessary, be slowed down. This process is known as *flow control*. We shall learn more about some methods of handling this problem in our discussion of TCP/IP.

# Connection-oriented and connectionless protocols

In data communications, we distinguish between two different types of protocol, the so-called *connection-oriented* and *connectionless* protocols. In the former case, a connection with the communication partner is generated before the data is exchanged, while in the latter case only individual messages are sent. Without going into further details of their advantages and disadvantages here (which are sometimes discussed with religious fervour by experts), the two types of protocol may usually be distinguished by the volume of their reliability functions (which in turn affects their efficiency). A connection-oriented protocol with many reliability functions usually has a higher computational processing requirement than a connectionless protocol. Table 1.2 lists the characteristics of both types of protocol.

**Table 1.2**   Types of protocol.

| Type | Mode of operation | Application areas |
| --- | --- | --- |
| Connection oriented | Three phases: connection set-up, data transfer, connection shutdown | Terminal sessions, bulk data transfer |
| Connectionless | Transport of self-contained messages, stateless | Directory services, databases, transaction systems |

The execution of message exchange in a connection-oriented protocol is similar to a telephone conversation. The data exchange only begins after the call partners have been introduced to each other and several formal exchanges have taken place. The connection is only broken off when both parties have agreed that the exchanged data is intelligible. Thus, connection-oriented protocols are also said to form *virtual circuits*. Virtual circuits, which from a UNIX programmer's view behave like a bidirectional pipe, are used when, in the context of the message exchange, it is important to maintain a connection over a relatively long period of time, or where data-transmission reliability plays a role. Several virtual (logical) connections may usually be maintained over a physical (real) line.

Information units in connectionless protocols are similar to telegrams, in that they usually form self-contained messages. Thus, these information units are also called *datagrams*. Connectionless protocols come to the fore in the transaction mode, for example, for database queries. Because of their stateless nature, connectionless protocols cannot provide such reliability features as flow control or retransmission of packets. If a more reliable service is required by an application, the quality of service of a connectionless protocol layer has to be augmented by a higher-ranking protocol layer. Examples of this are TCP on top of IP or the RPC protocol on top of UDP.

The transport layer of the TCP/IP architecture involves both types of protocol, with TCP as a connection-oriented protocol and UDP as a connectionless protocol (see Chapter 3). As we shall see later, IP is a connectionless protocol of the network layer.

# 2

# Genesis of the TCP/IP architecture

- The beginnings of ARPANET

- Goals of the TCP/IP architecture

- Comparison of OSI and TCP/IP architecture

- Importance of the Berkeley UNIX implementation

The TCP/IP architecture (sometimes also called Internet architecture) has, over recent years, moved from a shadowy presence in the world of established proprietary protocols to the centre of heterogeneous networking. Before going into the technical details of the associated protocols, let us take a brief look at the historical background of the overall TCP/IP architecture.

## The beginnings of ARPANET

At the end of the sixties, there was great demand at various US universities and research centres for a network to permit nation-wide utilization of their existing computer resources. In addition, it was also felt desirable to provide the researchers with a facility for data exchange. There was particular interest in practical experience of the design, implementation and use of network technology in general and of packet-switched networks in particular. To this end, the *Advanced Research Project Agency* (ARPA), a US government organization which later (from 1972) promoted primarily projects of military interest (and was thus renamed DARPA), formed the *ARPANET,* or the *DARPA Internet* as it is now known. In 1985, the Internet project was wound down.

Initially, ARPANET was a network of leased lines connected by special switching nodes, the so-called *Internet Message Processors* (IMPs). A host computer accessed ARPANET via connection to an IMP using the *1822* protocol. 1822 was the number of the *Internet Engineering Note* (IEN) in which the protocol was specified. Today, ARPANET is a subnetwork of the world-wide TCP/IP Internet; meanwhile, there exist hundreds of other large TCP/IP networks in research and industry, which are connected to one another.

The first proposal for ARPANET in Summer 1968 was initially for four IMPs at the University of California in Los Angeles (UCLA) and Santa Barbara (UCSB), the Stanford Research Institute (SRI) and the University of Utah. The contract was won in December 1968 by the company *Bolt, Beranek & Newman* (BBN). Over the following years, this company was to have a strong influence on the development of the TCP/IP architecture. Designs for the individual protocols and specific notions of what the ARPANET should achieve were developed, gradually at first. Demands existed for remote logins and file transfer (these two services came on top of the *Network Control Program* (NCP), the predecessor of TCP/IP). The TCP/IP collection of protocols was only developed later. ARPANET entered into regular use in 1971. In summary, it may be said that the success of ARPANET was determined by the uniform allocation of three services to all connected computers:

- remote login
- file transfer
- electronic mail.

At first, electronic mail was still integrated in FTP (see Chapter 4) and was thus a variant of the file transfer. Only later was an individual protocol provided for this service (SMTP, see Chapter 4). Today, most of the Internet traffic is mail oriented.

# Goals of the TCP/IP architecture

In 1973, it was clear that the protocols then used in the lower layers were functionally inadequate. Consequently, a project was initiated to propose a new protocol basis. The main features of TCP/IP and the gateway architecture were first laid down in an article by V. Cerf and R. Kahn in 1974. The goals of the architecture were then defined to be:

- Independence from the underlying network technology and from the architecture of the host computer.
- Universal connectivity throughout the network.
- End-to-end acknowledgements.
- Standardized application protocols.

Of these goals, at least the first two (namely, the requirement for heterogeneity on the host computer side and for the applicability of very different communication media or subnetworks) were unusual (in a world in which predominantly proprietary protocols were used). These properties are the reason why now, in the nineties, TCP/IP can establish itself as an OSI technology.

As previously mentioned, in the years 1983 to 1984, the US Department of Defence had already declared certain protocols of the TCP/IP architecture to be MIL-STDs and introduced them as criteria in tenders. Version 4 of TCP/IP, as found on UNIX computers, was standardized in 1981 in ARPANET through RFCs. The full transition from NCP to TCP/IP throughout ARPANET only occurred in 1982.

The main characteristics of the TCP/IP architecture which directly implement the above goals are:

- connectionless protocols in the network layer

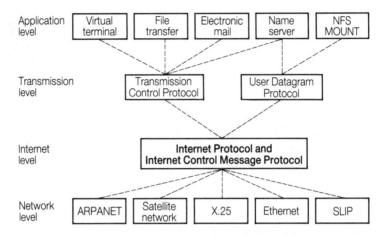

**Figure 2.1**   TCP/IP architecture model.

- nodes as packet-switching computers
- dynamic routing
- transport protocols with security functions
- a common set of application programs.

## Comparison of OSI and TCP/IP architecture

The OSI reference model was introduced in the last chapter. There is also a reference model for the TCP/IP architecture. Since experiences of TCP/IP projects have influenced OSI standardization, it is not surprising that the two models are in part quite similar. The model shown in Figure 2.1 is intended to provide an insight into the thought processes of the TCP/IP developers.

The differences between the OSI and the TCP/IP architectures relate primarily to the philosophy in the layers above the transport level. Here, the OSI model has two additional layers, the session layer and the presentation layer. TCP/IP architects, on the other hand, viewed the functions of the presentation and session layers as part of the application layer.

The requirement for independence from the transmission medium also resulted in the decision, at the network level of TCP/IP, to combine the later OSI physical and link layers. In TCP/IP jargon, the elements of the network level are termed subnetworks. In practice, the architectural solution is at this point thoroughly pragmatic, since the functions of the two lowest OSI layers will largely be implemented in a closed manner on intelligent (for example, Ethernet) controllers. In addition, the construction permits a self-contained network with its own nodes, protocol layers, gateways, etc., to be used as a subnetwork. Thus, for example, it is possible to operate TCP/IP over X.25 or any other network.

The requirement for universal connectivity is supported by the *Internet Protocol* (IP): at the network level of TCP/IP there is *only one* protocol which all participating hosts and nodes can understand. The *Internet Control Message Protocol* (ICMP), a component of every IP implementation, transports error and diagnostic information for IP.

At the transport level, in addition to the *Transmission Control Protocol* (TCP) and the *User Datagram Protocol* (UDP), other protocols are also operated in the Internet, mostly for research purposes. However, TCP and UDP are the two most common protocols.

# Importance of the Berkeley UNIX implementation

The success of TCP/IP in the UNIX world was largely a result of the fact that the University of California in Berkeley undertook an implementation of TCP/IP on behalf of DARPA for its UNIX systems – namely, the famous 4.2BSD (*Berkeley System Distribution*) – and that the source code of this implementation was made available as *public domain software* in September 1983. Legally, research results and developments of American universities belong to the American people: they are available to anyone for a nominal fee, provided that the originator's copyright is recognized. For this reason, practically all TCP/IP implementations under UNIX are based on the Berkeley code. Moreover, many manufacturers of non-UNIX systems and intelligent peripherals have also referred back to the Berkeley basis. Since this results in the use of only one interpretation of the specifications, there are no problems associated with the use of systems from different manufacturers.

Meanwhile, there are new versions of the BSD system in which the implementation of the TCP/IP architecture is both corrected and improved: most of the TCP/IP implementations available today contain, in some form, either the modifications or the whole code of 4.3BSD as released in April 1986. Further optimizations of the TCP implementation were released in the so-called 4.3BSD/Tahoe version in June 1988.

# 3

# TCP/IP – layers 1 to 4

- General specifications

- Internet Protocol

- Transmission Control Protocol

- User Datagram Protocol

- Internet Control Message Protocol

- Ethernet and IEEE 802.3

- Serial Line IP

- X.25

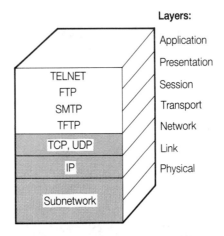

**Figure 3.1**  The lower protocol layers of the TCP/IP architecture.

In this chapter, we are concerned with the protocols of the TCP/IP architecture in the lower layers, up to and including the transport layer.

In Figure 3.1, these layers are marked in the OSI reference model. We begin with the Internet Protocol (IP), since it is the central protocol in the architecture. From here, we move a layer upwards to the transport protocols, the Transmission Control Protocol (TCP) and the User Datagram Protocol (UDP), which together with the Internet Protocol exist in all systems and are independent of the transmission medium. Finally, a short section is devoted to the Internet Control Message Protocol (ICMP). Equipped with the necessary tools, we then consider the most commonly used transmission media in UNIX systems and their associated protocols.

In the discussion of protocol attributes, we shall describe the construction of protocol headers and the addressing in the different layers. Then we shall consider several algorithms which may be used to increase the efficiency of the implementation.

| 0 | 7 | 15 | 31 |
|---|---|---|---|
| 1 | 2 | 3 | 4 |
| 5 | 6 | . . . | |

**Figure 3.2** Byte sequence in protocol headers.

# General specifications

Not all computer architectures encode data in the same way; thus, the exchange of packets with protocol fields between such systems necessitates the determination of a uniform format for these fields. The same is true of user data; however, this problem is described in full in the section on the XDR protocol in the chapter on NFS protocols (Chapter 9). For the moment, we shall restrict ourselves to the protocol headers:

- Since TCP/IP protocol fields contain both single bits and integers, the bit and byte order is defined to be *big-endian*, with the element of lowest order at the lowest order position.

- An integer consisting of several bytes is sent with the highest order byte first (see Figure 3.2).

# Internet Protocol

The Internet Protocol (IP) is the corner-stone of the TCP/IP architecture and is specified in both RFC 791 (Postel, 1981a) and MIL-STD 1777 (DOD, 1983a). All computers in Internet understand IP. The main tasks of IP are the addressing of the computers and the fragmentation of packets; it contains no functions for end-to-end message reliability or for flow control. IP makes the 'best effort' to forward packets to the next destination, although this forwarding is not guaranteed. Before we begin our discussion of the protocol header, here is a brief summary of the main attributes of IP:

- connectionless protocol
- fragments (divides) packets if necessary

**Figure 3.3**   IP protocol header.

- addressing via 32-bit Internet addresses
- 8-bit transport protocol addresses
- maximum packet size of 65535 bytes
- contains only a header checksum, no data checksum
- protocol fields which are not always required are optional
- finite packet lifetime
- 'best-effort' delivery.

The fields in the protocol header shown in Figure 3.3 have the following meaning:

## Version number

This 4-bit field contains the version number of IP, the current version number being 4.

## Length

This specifies the length of the IP protocol header in 32-bit words. The shortest IP protocol header contains five words; since, as is normally the case, almost all TCP/IP packets begin with $45_{(16)}$. The length of the protocol header may be increased by the addition of optional fields, whence for the purposes of interpretation, the exact length must be known.

| Bits | If 0 | If 1 |
|------|------|------|
| 0–2 | Precedence | |
| 3 | Normal delay | Low delay |
| 4 | Normal throughput | High throughput |
| 5 | Normal reliability | High reliability |
| 6–7 | Reserved | |

```
0   1   2   3   4   5   6   7
+-----------+---+---+---+---+---+
| Precedence| D | T | R | 0 | 0 |
+-----------+---+---+---+---+---+
```

**Figure 3.4**   Structure of the service type field.

## Type of service

Entries for protocol devices to process the message according to set criteria. Figure 3.4 shows the detailed structure of this field. In practice, the value 0 is almost always used since qualitatively different paths between two computers seldom exist. Moreover, as far as is known, no UNIX IP implementation evaluates entries in this field (this may be because there is no program interface to fill the field).

## Packet length

This contains the length of the packet including the protocol header. This entry is used to establish the data length and is later passed to the transport protocol in the so-called pseudo header. Since this is only a 16-bit field, an IP packet (including the header) may have a maximum length of 65535 bytes ($2^{16}$). The IP specification states that any host must be capable of receiving and reassembling (that is, putting together again) packets of up to 576 bytes in length, which corresponds to 512 data bytes plus additional protocol headers. As a rule, computers are able to process much larger packets, at least up to the maximum size for the networks to which they are attached (for example, an Ethernet packet).

## Identification

This is a unique identifier (for example, a counter) which is created by the sending host. This field is used in the reassembly of fragments to identify all the pieces of a fragment chain.

### Flags

Two bits, DF (Don't Fragment) and MF (More Fragments), control the handling of packets in the case of fragmentation. If the DF bit is set, the IP packet is not to be fragmented under any circumstances, even if it can no longer be forwarded and must be discarded. The MF bit shows whether or not the IP packet is followed by more subpackets. The first bit of this field is unused. The fragmentation algorithm is described in more detail later in the chapter.

### Fragment offset

If the MF bit is set, the fragment offset contains the position of the submessage contained in this packet, relative to the beginning of the whole message. The receiving host can use this entry to reassemble the original packet correctly. Since, because of the flags described above, this is only a 13-bit field, the offset must be counted in units of 8 bytes and the maximum length of an IP packet is thus $8 * 2^{13} = 65535$.

### Time to live

Here, the sending host specifies how long the packet may remain in the network before it must be discarded. RFC 791 (Postel, 1981a) specifies the units used in this field, in seconds, and dictates that every node must decrease this field by at least 1 even if the processing time is less than one second. Thus, the time to live (TTL) is usually equal to the maximum number of nodes that a packet may pass through. If this field contains 0, the packet must be discarded by the current processor: this prevents a packet from circulating endlessly in the network. In this case, the sender of the packet receives an ICMP message about this event. As a rule, UNIX machines set this field to a value between 15 (4.2BSD) and 30 (4.3BSD). Old 4.2BSD-based IP implementations reduce the field by 5, while new versions reduce it by 1 only.

### Transport protocol

This contains the ID of the transport protocol to which the packet has to be handed over. For example, for TCP, this number is 6, for UDP the number is 17 and for ICMP the number is 1. These numbers are determined by the NIC in regular RFCs (Postel and Reynolds, 1987). Currently, there are approximately 50 official higher protocols.

### Header checksum

This field contains the checksum for the protocol header fields. Control checks prevent nodes or hosts from working with false data. For efficiency, user data in the IP packet is not checked; this check is carried out by the recipient within the transport protocol. Since the IP packet is altered at every node by a decrease in the TTL field, it is important that the checksum is created very efficiently. The so-called *Internet checksum*, for all protocols in the TCP/IP architecture in which checksums are used, is given by: *the 1s complement of the 16-bit sum of all 16-bit words of the data to be checked.*

This algorithm is simple and fast; it is a prerequisite for the efficient operation of nodes. The error-detection ability of the Internet checksum is however limited: since it only involves simple addition, it would not, for example, detect missing 16-bit words which only contain zeros. However, the data checksums of TCP and UDP cover other entries (length, sender, etc.) in addition to the data, so that undetected data loss is practically ruled out.

## Source and destination addresses

The 32-bit Internet addresses, whose structure will be described in detail in the following pages, are entered here.

## Options and padding

For special tasks (network management, security), the IP protocol header is extended to include options which we shall consider later. So that the number of 16-bit words in the IP protocol header is always a multiple of 4 (we recall the header-length field), padding characters must be inserted, if necessary.

## Addressing at the IP level

The addressing of a communication partner, such as an application program, requires four different addresses when passing through the first four protocol layers:

(1) A subnetwork address (for example, an Ethernet address).

(2) An Internet address.

(3) A transport protocol address.

(4) A port number.

Two of these addresses, the Internet address and the transport protocol

**Figure 3.5**   Internet address types.

address, are given in fields in the IP protocol header. The more important of these two addresses is the *Internet address*, which is a 32-bit field. It is more important because every Internet node has one or more unique addresses of this type and part of the packet-forwarding service provided by IP involves the use of fields in the Internet address.

As shown in Figure 3.5, there are three address classes with *network* and *host computer identifiers* of different lengths. The network ID defines the network in which a computer is situated: all computers in the same network have the same network ID. The host ID identifies a specific computer within this network. Host IDs whose bits are all set to 0 or 1 are reserved for special functions and should not be assigned.

Why are there three types of Internet address? The explanation is simple: when ARPANET began there were only *class A* addresses, since it was assumed that there would only be a few large networks. With the introduction of local area networks in many organizations, it was soon clear that this assumption was no longer tenable and it was decided to introduce two further types, namely, class B and class C addresses: *class C* for small networks with few hosts and *class B* for medium-sized networks. For several years, experiments have been carried out with so-called *multicast addresses*, in which IP packets with a *class D* address are simultaneously distributed to a group of hosts (a precise description of the mechanism is given in RFC 1054 (Deering, 1988)). *Class E* addresses are currently reserved for research purposes.

**Figure 3.6**   Schematic example of a multi-homing host.

However, there are advantages and disadvantages in the fact that the Internet address consists of a host ID and a network ID:

- The Internet address provides an unambiguous description of the access to a host in the network; thus, the gateways do not need to manage a host–network assignment table. Consequently, given the Internet address, the nodes can immediately make their routing decisions without first having to take time to determine the network number of a host.

- If a host is connected to another network, its Internet address is different.

- If a host is connected to several networks (so-called *multi-homing host*), it has several Internet addresses and thus several names, as shown in Figure 3.6.

- If only one of several connections fails, the host cannot be reached at this address, even though access via intact connections may still be possible.

## Subnetwork routing

RFC 950 (Mogul and Postel, 1985) introduced a convention to facilitate routing in large subnetworks. In this convention, the host ID part of the Internet address is further subdivided into a subnetwork number and the station number proper. The subnetwork number may be used to branch into internal subordinate networks within the subnetwork; outwardly the whole network appears as a unit.

Figure 3.7 gives an example of a class B address with an 8-bit field for the subnetwork ID. The size and position of the subnetwork ID are not fixed, the size depending on the number of addressable subnetworks and the number of hosts per subnetwork. Both must be fixed for the whole

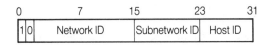

**Figure 3.7**   Class B address with field for subnetwork ID.

network by the network administrator. Readers are strongly recommended to adopt the position between the network and host IDs as shown in Figure 3.7 and the ordering as for a single field.

As a rule, UNIX hosts support subnetwork routing, at least all TCP/IP implementations based on 4.3BSD. The TCP/IP system must be told which bits of the Internet address form the network address; this is done using a network mask via the command *ifconfig*. For example, for the address shown in Figure 3.7, the network mask would be FF.FF.FF.00$_{(16)}$, whereas without a subnetwork it would be FF.FF.00.00$_{(16)}$. When looking for a network to forward a packet into, the routing algorithm in the gateway simply uses the remaining bits after a logical AND-operation with the mask on the original address.

## Internet addresses in practice

In practice, only addresses of classes A to C are used. Figure 3.8 shows examples of various address types, again as used in actual networks. The network ID is in **bold** type; the remaining bytes contain the host ID.

When a host is connected to a network, the network and the host IDs must be assigned. If the host is to be integrated into a network that already exists, the complete Internet address should be allocated by a network administrator, to avoid overlap with other hosts. If a new network is to be constructed, prior consideration should be given to whether it is to operate later in association with other networks. In this case, it is advisable to choose a suitable, non-colliding network ID immediately, since later changes are always very expensive. In as much as network IDs are not prescribed externally, each of the three classes A to C may be used. The only point to note here is the maximum number of addressable hosts per class: 255 for class C against up to 16 million for class A. If a very large network is planned, the address should be chosen so that subnetwork addressing is possible.

Class A
$10.0.0.32_{(10)} = $ **00001010.00000000.00000000.00010000**$_{(2)}$

Class B
$128.14.58.60_{(10)} = $ **10000000.00001110.**00111010.00111100$_{(2)}$

Class C
$192.9.150.202_{(10)} = $ **11000000.00001001.10010110.**11001010$_{(2)}$

**Figure 3.8**    Examples of Internet addresses.

In allocating Internet addresses, you should also bear in mind that network and host IDs with all bits set to 0 or 1 are reserved and that, in addition, network ID 127 is reserved for the internal loopback network (see Chapter 6).

## Fragmentation

In order to transmit packets over any type of network, IP must be capable of adapting the sizes of its datagrams to each network. Thus, for example, *CCITT X.25* packets should not be larger than 128 bytes, while an Ethernet packet may transport up to 1526 bytes of data. It goes without saying that data transport in the subnetwork should also be efficient.

To achieve this, it is not however sufficient that the transport protocols, such as TCP or UDP, are themselves only able to generate small packets. Since a packet, en route from the source to the destination, may, in certain cases, pass through several different networks with different maximum packet sizes and since, moreover, this route may vary from packet to packet within a TCP connection, a flexible procedure must be applied: *fragmentation.*

Fragmentation means that the IP of each node in the network should be capable of dividing a received packet, in order to transmit it over a subnetwork to the next node or host. Every destination IP should be capable of reassembling fragmented messages.

## Fragmentation process

Every fragment of a message contains its own complete IP protocol header together with the identification field for the initial message, which may be

**Figure 3.9** Fragmentation of an IP packet.

used to recognize all the fragments of a message. Individual fragments of a message may reach their destination over different routes. The position of the data of a fragment within the whole message is communicated using the fragment offset field.

Figure 3.9 shows a schematic representation of a fragmented IP packet. If a recipient has to forward a message fragment further, it may either forward the individual fragments unaltered or reassemble the whole message. Thus, in certain cases, another, possibly optimal, packet size may be provided for the next network. This is certainly only possible if the recipient can be sure that it will receive the entire message (for example, on point-to-point links). If the source processor wishes to prevent the packet from being fragmented, possibly because the destination is not capable of reassembling it, it may set the DF bit in the IP protocol header.

The following example shows the contents of various protocol fields during the course of fragmentation. Note that the fragment offset is measured in units of 8 bytes; thus, all packets except the final packet must have a length divisible by 8 (in our case, 104 bytes). The whole of the data and the IP protocol header of length 20 bytes give a total length of 124 bytes.

*Initial situation:*

- Network maximum packet length: 128 bytes.
- Number of data bytes to be sent: 300 bytes.
- Packet identification: 2354.
- DF bit not set.
- No options.

*Result after fragmentation:*

- Fragment 1: length 124, offset 0, MF bit = 1, ID = 2354.
- Fragment 2: length 124, offset 13, MF bit = 1, ID = 2354.
- Fragment 3: length 112, offset 26, MF bit = 0, ID = 2354.

When the first fragment of a message reaches the destination, a watchdog timer is set. If the watchdog timer terminates before the remaining fragments arrive, the incomplete message is discarded. This prevents incomplete messages from reserving unnecessary buffer storage when fragments have been lost. If the sender is nonetheless interested in the delivery of the message, it will usually repeat it after a certain time (for example, for TCP after the termination of the acknowledgement timer). The reassembly timer in IP on UNIX systems is usually set to 30 seconds.

## Options

In IP datagrams the so-called *IP options* are also sent as an extension to the IP protocol header. This optional extension was chosen so that it is not always necessary to reserve space for rarely used fields and so that the IP protocol header is kept as small as possible. The list of the available IP options is as follows:

### Source route

The IP protocol header is followed by a list of Internet addresses through which the datagram must pass. Thus, a specific route may be prescribed. Here, we differentiate between a *strict source and record route* and a *loose source and record route*. In the first case, the nodes must follow the given path exactly, while in the second case any intermediate stations may be used.

### Record route

The nodes which the datagram passes through are instructed to return their Internet addresses. Thus, we may determine the route taken by a datagram.

### Time stamp

The time of passage through the nodes is returned, so that, for example, delays on sections may be measured. If at the same time a list of Internet addresses is requested, a specific route can then also be preset.

### Security

Here, directions for handling the packets according to security requirements are laid down. This option was included in IP for military purposes and is only supported by a few commercial implementations. The most recent specification of this option may be found in RFC 1038 (St. Johns, 1988).

### Stream identifier

This is an outdated option which should be ignored.

### End-of-option list

This indicates the end of the list of options.

### No operation

This may be used to pad out the option list.

Options consist of either a single byte with the option identifier or a combination of identifier, length field and data. Should entries in the options be recorded by nodes, the sender must reserve sufficient room for the option data in the IP protocol header. This prevents the IP protocol header from expanding and avoids data being copied from one area to another to make room for option data. In this case, a pointer points to the next available space in the options. Further details may be found in RFC 791 (Postel, 1981a).

Usually, UNIX implementations support all the above options with the exception of security and stream identifier.

RFC 1063 (Mogul *et al.*, 1988) proposes a *probe MTU option* to determine the least *Maximum Transfer Unit* (MTU) on a route. This information enables a transport protocol to generate an optimal packet length and thus prevent additional fragmentation. Suppose that an IP datagram with this option is sent. The nodes passed through by the IP packet enter the MTU of the next subnetwork in a field provided for this purpose, whenever the MTU is less than the value already contained in that field. The recipient generates and returns a response datagram. This option is also expected to be supported by UNIX systems in the future.

## Transmission Control Protocol

The Transmission Control Protocol (TCP) is a protocol of the transport layer, and thus lies above IP. Its main task is the reliable transportation of data through the network. TCP is specified in RFC 793 (Postel, 1981c) and in MIL-STD 1778 (DOD, 1983b). Its transport address in the IP protocol header is 6. Briefly, the main attributes of TCP are:

- Provides a fully duplex bidirectional virtual circuit.
- As seen by the user, data is transmitted as a data stream (not in blocks).
- Reliable data transmission using:
  - sequence numbers
  - checksums
  - acknowledgements
  - segment retransmission after acknowledgement timeout.
- Sliding-window principle for greater efficiency.
- Urgent data and push function.
- Transport-user addressing using 16-bit port number.
- Graceful connection shutdown.

The functionality of TCP is not very different from other complicated transport protocols (such as ISO-TP4) except for the fact that block boundaries are not preserved. The reason for this difference in behaviour is the byte-oriented nature of TCP: nearly all the fields used in the protocol header are calculated in bytes and not in blocks. This allows a flexible dimensioning of blocks. Data is transmitted in the form of blocks (in TCP jargon: segments); however, the size of the segment in the network is determined by parameters such as network load, window size or the resources of one of the partners. Thus, given these variable segments, it would be very expensive to preserve the distribution over blocks as generated originally by the user (or in some cases randomly). Experience also shows that it is not absolutely necessary to preserve block boundaries in the transport layer and that this may be undertaken by functions in other layers (for example, in the session layer).

Figure 3.10 shows the structure of the TCP protocol header. The fields included have the following significance:

### Source and destination port numbers

Two 16-bit fields which denote the end points at both ends of a virtual circuit. We shall discuss the significance of the port number in more detail later in the chapter.

**Figure 3.10**   TCP protocol header.

## Sequence and acknowledgement numbers

Each of these is a 32-bit word which gives the position of the data within the data stream exchanged during the connection. The sequence number refers to the send direction and the acknowledgement number applies to the number of bytes received by the other end. On connection set-up, each partner of a TCP connection generates an initial sequence number whose most important property must be that it is not repeated within the period during which a packet may remain in the network (IP time to live). These numbers are exchanged and acknowledged on connection set-up. On data transfer, the sequence number is increased by the sender by the number of bytes already sent. In the acknowledgement number, the recipient states how many bytes of the message have been correctly received. The large numerical range of $2^{32}$ provides sufficient protection against duplication and overlap, since on overflow sequence numbers start again at 0.

## Data offset

This entry contains the length of the TCP protocol header in 32-bit words to determine the start of the data.

## *Flags*

These bits are used to trigger actions in TCP. If they are set to 1, this means that:

| Name | Explanation |
|------|-------------|
| URG | Pointer in *Urgent* field is valid. |
| ACK | Acknowledgement number is valid. |
| PSH | Data in this segment should be passed immediately to the application: an acknowledgement for this segment means that all data up to this acknowledgement number has reached the communication partner. UNIX implementations always send PSH when they send all the remaining data in the send buffer with the segment. |
| RST | Resetting of the connection or response to an invalid segment. |
| SYN | Connection set-up request, segment must be acknowledged. |
| FIN | One-sided connection shutdown and end of the data flow from this direction, segment must be acknowledged. |

## *Window size*

This contains the number of bytes that the recipient is able to receive in its data buffers for this connection (*receive window*). The destination TCP uses this entry to control the data flow: a window size of 0 would, for example, effectively stop the source TCP. The data flow is restarted by gradually increasing the window size. The maximum window size is 2048 bytes in 4.2BSD and 4096 bytes in 4.3BSD. Optimal determination of the window size during data transfer is one of the most complicated algorithms of a TCP implementation.

TCP works on the *sliding-window* principle: each party to a connection may send the number of bytes specified in the window, without having to wait for an acknowledgement from the other party. During the send process, acknowledgements of receipt of the data by the other party (which may again simultaneously set new window sizes) may be simultaneously received. This means that the sender does not have to wait for the corresponding acknowledgement after each segment.

Simple protocols without a window mechanism send (for example) a data block at any given time and then wait for an acknowledgement before sending another block. It is clear that this cannot provide a satisfactory data throughput rate, for example, on a satellite circuit with several seconds elapsed time, and that valuable transmission bandwidth is lost.

**Figure 3.11**   TCP and UDP pseudo header.

Simultaneous send-and-acknowledge achieves a parallelism which produces an optimal throughput rate even on subnetworks with a higher elapsed time.

### Checksum

The checksum is applied to the protocol header, the data and the *pseudo header*. As in all other protocols described here, the same algorithm as used to generate the IP checksum is used to generate the TCP checksum.

In the pseudo header shown in Figure 3.11, a number of fields from the IP protocol header are delivered to the transport protocol together with the data segment. These are included in the TCP checksum calculation for the segment and should, in addition to providing the information contained, prevent packets from being incorrectly forwarded by IP. Moreover, a check for undetected data loss is also possible, using the length entry (see the description of the IP checksum).

On the sender side, a pseudo header is also generated on creation of the TCP checksum and is included in the checksum. The data in the pseudo header is however not transferred in this form in the segment.

### Urgent pointer

Together with the sequence number, this is a pointer to a data byte. This data byte is the end of a message section where the following data is identified as being important. This function is termed *urgent data*. Since this mechanism is somewhat unusual and complicated, a separate section

**Table 3.1**  Analogy between Internet addresses and phone numbers.

| Internet socket | Telephone |
|---|---|
| Network number | Area code |
| Host ID | Phone number |
| Port number | Extension |

has been devoted to it in the following pages, so as to provide more details of the function and its application.

## Options

TCP has only three options: End-of-Option List, No Operation and Maximum Segment Size. The latter is sent on connection set-up to indicate readiness to receive segments larger than 536 bytes. As a rule, UNIX systems cater for segment sizes between 1024 bytes (4.2BSD) and the maximum network packet length (4.3BSD).

## Port numbers

As already noted, port numbers are used for addressing at the transport level. Since port numbers are 16-bit fields, a host computer may theoretically establish up to 65535 different TCP connections concurrently.

UDP also uses port numbers for addressing. Note however that TCP and UDP each have their own address space; thus, port number 511 in TCP is not identical to port number 511 in UDP. The range of validity of a port number is restricted to a host. Together the network number, the host ID and the port number determine a communication end point (or socket), similar to an extension of a telephone installation, as shown in Table 3.1.

Connection establishment over TCP proceeds as for the telephone; here too there is a passive partner (the person being called) and an active partner (the caller). Before two programs can communicate with one another, both must initialize communication end points, whose addresses are used in the protocol headers of the individual layers. So that they may be indeed connected together, the address of the passive partner must be known to the active partner; thus, both parties must have previously agreed upon a port number at which the passive partner (or *server*) should await the connection. The port number of the active partner (or *client*) is irrelevant, unless the server prescribes a special port number for the client.

Like the service department or the speaking clock in the telephone system, TCP/IP applications, such as, for example, *TELNET* or *FTP*, could be regarded as fixed services which are available at a given, well-known

**Table 3.2**   Extract from the list of fixed port numbers.

| Service | Port number | Protocol |
| --- | --- | --- |
| TELNET | 23 | TCP |
| FTP | 21 | TCP |
| SMTP | 25 | TCP |
| rlogin | 513 | TCP |
| rsh | 514 | TCP |
| portmap | 111 | TCP |
| rwhod | 513 | UDP |
| portmap | 111 | UDP |

number. In the TCP/IP world, such a number is called a *well-known port number*. Then we may say that: *every service must have its own fixed port number. The client addresses the server, which provides the service at this port number.*

Table 3.2 contains examples of some of the services available on UNIX machines, together with their port numbers and the protocol used for these services. These and other details are found in the file */etc/services*. As you will see, *rlogin* and *rwhod* use the same port number; but they do so without colliding, since one service is executed over TCP and the other over UDP. On the other hand, in the case of the NFS *portmap* program, the same service is offered over both protocols and for simplicity the same port number is used for both. The operation of several protocols is actually implemented in the server itself, since the latter opens a communication end point for each protocol used.

## Urgent data

Other protocols, such as the ISO transport protocols, contain a feature called *expedited data*.   This provides the possibility of sending urgent messages (usually of restricted length) to the communication partner over and above the normal data stream ('*out-band*'). This function is generally used to signal an unusual state, for example, program abortion or the like.

Urgent data is a different mechanism which is often wrongly compared with expedited data.   Unlike expedited data, in this case, the message is not preferentially transported; instead TCP signals to the receiving application that important data, which should be read immediately, is to be found at a certain point in the data stream

| TCP A | | TCP B |
|---|---|---|
| → | (SEQ = 100),(FLAGS = SYN) | |
| | (SEQ = 300),(ACK = 101),(FLAGS = SYN,ACK) | ← |
| → | (SEQ = 101),(ACK = 301),(FLAGS = ACK) | |

**Figure 3.12**   Connection in TCP.

('*in-band*'). The urgent pointer points to the last byte of the previous data, and the next byte is the start of the urgent message. It now falls to the receiving application to read the data at the position following the urgent pointer.

In UNIX systems, a signal may be sent to notify an application of the receipt of urgent data.

The urgent data mechanism was specially conceived for TELNET: the TELNET client uses it to send *synchc* events, upon which the TELNET server is instructed to discard all data queueing in the circuit and to look for TELNET protocol statements. In this way, for example, an urgent statement can be forcibly processed, even though the TELNET server has not processed all the input data prior to this statement.

## TCP scenarios

In this section, we shall show in three stages how TCP uses the fields of the TCP protocol header in the most important phases of a connection, namely, *connection establishment, data exchange* and *connection shutdown*. In the diagrams, the arrows always indicate the segment send direction. The fields of the TCP protocol header are given in brackets.

Figure 3.12 shows a connection. Here, there is a so-called *three-way handshake* in which each party, activated by the SYN flag, must acknowledge the other party's sequence number by increasing it by 1. The sequence number (SEQ = 100) of TCP A is found in the response of TCP B in the acknowledgement field (ACK = 101), and vice versa. The ACK flag indicates that the value in the acknowledgement field is valid.

Figure 3.13 shows a data exchange which is taking place in both directions simultaneously. Note how the destination always acknowledges by entering the sequence number in the SEQ field (SEQ = 101) increased by the number of data bytes received (DATA = 5) in the ACK field (ACK = 106). Data is sent in the opposite direction together with the acknowledgement and is acknowledged in the same way.

```
TCP A                                                              TCP B
→           (SEQ = 101),(ACK = 301),(FLAGS = ACK),(DATA = 5)
            (SEQ = 301),(ACK = 106),(FLAGS = ACK),(DATA = 10)        ←
→                (SEQ = 106),(ACK = 311),(FLAGS = ACK)
```

**Figure 3.13**   Data exchange in TCP.

Figure 3.14 shows how the connection is shut down on one side when TCP A sends a FIN flag. TCP acknowledges the FIN flag by increasing the sequence number (SEQ = 106) in the response segment by 1 (ACK = 107). This acknowledges the receipt of all data sent by TCP A up to that time. After that, no more data should be sent by TCP A. However, TCP B may continue to send until it itself sends a FIN flag.

While during connection establishment one party is active and the other passive, during data exchange and connection shutdown initiatives both partners have equal rights.

## Timers

In all protocols, a great deal of consideration is given not only to the protocol elements but also to the algorithms and the associated operations. Thus, in all protocol implementations timers are used to monitor the different operations. In this section, we shall consider the functions of these timers in TCP implementations in more detail.

```
TCP A                                                              TCP B
→               (SEQ = 106),(FLAGS = FIN,ACK)
               (SEQ = 311),(ACK = 107),(FLAGS = ACK)                ←
        (SEQ = 311),(ACK = 107),(FLAGS = ACK),(DATA = 5)            ←
→              (SEQ = 107),(ACK = 316),(FLAGS = ACK)
              (SEQ = 316),(ACK = 107),(FLAGS = FIN,ACK)             ←
→              (SEQ = 107),(ACK = 317),(FLAGS = ACK)
```

**Figure 3.14**   Connection shutdown in TCP.

$$\text{SRTT:} \ S = \alpha S + (1 - \alpha)R$$
$$\text{RTO:} \ T = \min(U, \max(L, \beta S))$$

**Key**

$S \equiv$ Smoothed round trip time

$R \equiv$ Round trip time

$T \equiv$ Retransmission timeout (for example, 30 seconds)

$U \equiv$ Maximum time limit (for example, 1 second)

$\alpha \equiv$ Smoothing factor (for example, 0.9)

$\beta \equiv$ Scaling factor (for example, 2.0)

**Figure 3.15**    Calculation of SRTT.

## Retransmission timeout

The *Retransmission Timeout* (RTO) is set off when the prescribed time interval between the sending of a TCP packet and the receipt of the corresponding acknowledgement is exceeded. In this case, the packet must be resent. In fact, the time interval should not be fixed, since otherwise TCP could not be operated over networks with different elapsed times. If, for example, we compare Ethernet with a serial connection via several gateways, the transmission rates differ by a factor of a thousand. Thus, for every packet in TCP, the time between transmission and receipt of an acknowledgement (the so-called *Round Trip Time* (RTT)) is measured. This measurement is fed into a formula that filters out peaks and troughs but also gradually adjusts to an extended or reduced elapsed time. The result is the *Smoothed Round Trip Time* (SRTT), being the mean elapsed time for segment exchange. This time is again scaled to allow for unforeseen delays.

Figure 3.15 shows both formulae specified by RFC 793: firstly, the SRTT filter, then the calculation of the RTO. If, after the retransmission of a segment, the retransmission timer again goes off, the RTO is usually increased exponentially up to 12 times. The connection is only deemed to be disrupted when this increase has no effect.

## Persistence timer

In data exchange over TCP, it is in principle possible for the receive window to be exactly 0 and for a segment intended to re-open the window to be lost at that exact same instant. As a result, both TCPs then go into an infinite wait for each other. A countermeasure against this is the persistence timer, which sends small TCP segments (1 byte) at set time intervals to check whether the receiving party is ready again. If, as before, the window size

**Table 3.3**   TCP timer settings (implementation dependent).

| Timer | Setting (seconds) |
|---|---|
| Retransmission timeout | Dynamic |
| Persistence timer | 5 |
| Quiet timer | 30 |
| Keep-alive timer | 45 |
| Idle timer | 360 |

is 0, a negative acknowledgement is returned; if the window size is larger, further data may be sent after the positive acknowledgement.

## Quiet timer

The designers of TCP were very careful people who wished to prevent any possible confusion of connections due to out-of-date TCP segments wandering about in the network (this possibility was distinctly possible in a network of the scale planned). Thus, after TCP connection shutdown, port numbers are only released after a fixed time interval of twice the *Maximum Segment Lifetime* (MSL) has elapsed. The MSL corresponds to the time in the TTL field used by IP.

The UNIX user notices this waiting time when he re-opens a connection between the same two partners (same port numbers) immediately after a shutdown. The system tells him that the port number used is still busy. A new connection set-up is only possible after approximately 30 seconds.

## Keep-alive timer and idle timer

Here, we are concerned with two timers which were not foreseen in the original TCP specification, but which are implemented in UNIX systems. Both are related. The keep-alive timer has the effect that an empty packet is sent at regular intervals to check that the connection to the other TCP still exists. If the partner TCP does not reply, the connection is broken off after execution of the idle timer. An application activates this timer with the KEEP_ALIVE option via the socket interface.

The values of the timers are given in Table 3.3. Note that the duration of the timer is implementation dependent and need not always be set to the values given. The values given here are from UNIX implementations up to and including 4.3BSD.

## Algorithms to increase efficiency

A TCP implementation 'according to the specification' and a high-grade optimized TCP subsystem, as found in UNIX systems, are very different. Countless improvements have been made to UNIX TCP implementations over recent years and many new algorithms have been integrated into 4.2BSD, 4.3BSD and subsequent versions, as described briefly here.

### Acknowledgement delay

This is a veteran that was already present in 4.2BSD. Normally, the destination TCP immediately sends a response segment, which reduces the window size and acknowledges the data, after a segment is received. After the data is copied to the receiving process, the system data buffers are freed, with the result that a segment to increase the window size is sent. When the program has processed the data, usually a response follows shortly; thus, one transaction requires three segments.

It has been shown that in many cases, for example, in TELNET operation, it is advantageous to delay the acknowledgement segment by two tenths of a second. After this brief period, all three items of information (window size, acknowledgement and response) may be sent in a single segment. So as not to slow down data transfers requiring a high throughput rate, the delay is omitted when a receive window is changed by at least 35% or two maximum segments.

### Silly window syndrome avoidance

In certain circumstances, receive-window entries are sent which are so small that the network and the computer are overloaded with the many acknowledgement segments. To prevent this, the receive window is only expanded when sufficient space is available (more than a quarter of the data buffer or a maximum segment). Conversely, the sender TCP behaves in a conservative way and only sends if the window provided is sufficiently large.

### Nagle algorithm or small packet avoidance

Named after its inventor John Nagle, this algorithm attempts to prevent the sending of small TCP segments. In this case, it is a question, on the sender side, of preventing data presented to TCP in small units by the application from being forwarded in this form. A first segment is sent immediately, while further data on the sender side is buffered until either a full maximum segment can be sent or an acknowledgement for the first segment is received. There are problems with this algorithm for applications which send many small messages (such as the X window system). In this case, the Nagle algorithm can be deactivated in a connection-dependent way.

### Slow start with congestion avoidance

These related algorithms, sometimes also called the Jacobson algorithms, have only recently become known and are mainly important for slow networks and for the operation of networks with gateways.

Over recent years, it had been noticed that as its load increased the Internet delivered an increasingly lower throughput and, indeed to some extent, more or less broke down. When the processes were considered in more detail, it was established that more than half the packets in the network were retransmissions of lost TCP segments. What had happened? A network path (here from the sender's data buffer, possibly via gateways, to the destination) can only carry a finite amount of data. When a gateway or a host is heavily loaded with traffic, it may happen that there is insufficient buffer space available in which to enter segments. In this case, the segments are discarded by the gateway, whereupon the sender of the packet decides to send a retransmission after the RTO has elapsed, and consequently the total network load again increases unnecessarily. The slow-start algorithm now attempts to determine how much data may be en route to a destination at a given time without losses occurring. This is done by gradually increasing the transmitted data set until a point is reached at which there is an equal flow of data without retransmissions. Where previously the data set to be transmitted was determined by the size, now the storage capacity of the network path, the so-called *congestion window*, is the determining factor, where the congestion window is always smaller than or equal to the receive window. Once the congestion window has evened out, it is only altered again when the occurrence of retransmissions signals an increase in the network load; in this case, congestion avoidance comes into play. At the same time, attempts are made to use any resources which may be released by constant, careful expansion of the congestion window. Because of the conservative behaviour, the throughput may be increased by up to 30% and the number of retransmitted segments decreased by more than 50%.

In association with these two algorithms, the determination of the retransmission timeout is also improved. The new algorithm produces even faster changes in the round trip time; thus, additional packet retransmissions are avoided.

# User Datagram Protocol

The User Datagram Protocol (UDP) is a connectionless transport protocol. It is specified in RFC 768 (Postel, 1980) and its transport address is 17.

**Figure 3.16**    UDP protocol header.

Unlike TCP, UDP is a real lightweight. Its attributes are:

- connectionless
- addressing via port numbers
- data checksums
- very simple
- 'best-effort' forwarding.

The fields of the UDP protocol header as shown in Figure 3.16 are as follows:

## Source and destination port numbers

As in TCP, port numbers are the reference to the transport protocol users.

## Length

This is the length of the whole datagram, including the protocol header.

## Checksum

The Internet checksum involves the data, the protocol header and the pseudo header. If this field contains the value 0, the sender has not entered a checksum and the UDP recipient does not carry out a check. In the first versions of the 4.2BSD system, the UDP code contained an error which led to the generation of an incorrect UDP checksum. Since it was not checked on the receiving side either, the bug went undetected for some time. In later versions, this fault has been eliminated. Normally, no UDP checksums are created in SunOS and SunOS-based systems, since it is assumed that the underlying network (usually Ethernet) guarantees data integrity. Checksums may be switched on by altering an operating system variable (*udpcksum*).

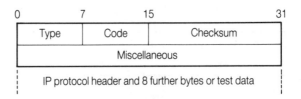

**Figure 3.17**   ICMP protocol header.

Over and above the work performed by IP, UDP only provides a port number and a data checksum. Unlike TCP, in this case, there are no transport acknowledgements or other reliability measures; however, the lack of these additions makes UDP particularly efficient and thus suitable for high-speed applications (for example, distributed file systems (NFS) or the like) which are, anyway, only suitable for installation on fast, reliable transmission media, as, for example, in *Local Area Networks* (LANs).

## Internet Control Message Protocol

Errors occur from time to time in all networks and nodes. These must be notified to those responsible or to those concerned. The notification is the responsibility of the Internet Control Message Protocol (ICMP) which is specified in RFC 792 (Postel, 1981b). ICMP is a component part of every IP implementation and in its role as a transport protocol its only tasks are to transport error and diagnostic data for IP. Its transport protocol address in the IP protocol header is 1.

Since ICMP has to transport various information, only the basic structure of the ICMP protocol header is fixed, the meaning of the individual fields being variable.

The structure shown in Figure 3.17, which is common to all ICMP messages, contains the following fields:

### Type

This specifies the type of the ICMP message. Table 3.4 gives a list of types.

Table **3.4** ICMP packet types.

| Type field | Function |
| --- | --- |
| 0 | Echo reply |
| 3 | Destination unreachable |
| 4 | Source quench |
| 5 | Redirect |
| 8 | Echo request |
| 11 | Time exceeded for a datagram |
| 12 | Parameter problem on a datagram |
| 13 | Time stamp request |
| 14 | Time stamp reply |

## Code

A further code which indicates subfunctions within a type.

## Checksum

This contains the Internet checksum for the complete ICMP message.

## Miscellaneous

This is a 32-bit field which contains information for miscellaneous purposes (sequence number, Internet addresses, etc.).

## IP protocol header

This contains the triggering IP datagram and the first 8 bits of the message transported in it. If the ICMP message is triggered by a message from TCP or UDP, the application program can be determined from the first 8 bytes of the TCP or UDP protocol header and an error message sent (for example, that the server port number specified in the connection request is not active in the target processor). This field may also be used to contain test data (for example, in echo request).

ICMP messages are initiated and processed internally by both IP and TCP and UDP. They should never be generated in response to another ICMP message or a broadcast, otherwise an endless loop might arise.

# ICMP packet types

Since the following ICMP packet types are implemented on all UNIX systems, we shall consider them in detail.

### Destination unreachable

Forwards a message reporting the following errors:

(1) Network, host, protocol or port unobtainable. The user program is sent a corresponding error message.

(2) Fragmentation required, but the DF bit was set.

(3) Source route option unsuccessful (see IP options).

### Source quench

If a gateway does not have the capacity to buffer a message, it may send this ICMP message to the responsible host. The transmitting host must then reduce the rate at which subsequent messages are sent. From 4.3BSD, this message is reacted to in TCP; in 4.2BSD it was simply ignored. In systems with congestion avoidance, the congestion window is decreased. UDP also ignores the message, in which case the sender's application program should be informed.

### Redirect

This is sent when a gateway recognizes that the sender of an IP packet could send the packet directly to the next gateway (thus an unnecessary detour is being made). The ICMP message contains the Internet address of the next direct gateway, which is entered into the sender's routing table.

### Echo reply and echo request

An *echo request* is sent to a computer and an *echo reply* follows as a consequence. The echo request and the echo reply are used to implement such practical functions as verification of operational readiness or measurement of elapsed time. Test data of arbitrary length is sent in the ICMP message in place of an IP protocol header; this data is returned in the echo reply.

### Time exceeded

This message is sent to a sender whose IP datagram had to be discarded on expiry of its TTL or for whose message the fragment reassembly timer has terminated.

### Parameter problem

The sender of an IP datagram is informed that, due to faulty entries in the IP protocol header, the packet has had to be discarded.

In RFC 950 (Mogul and Postel, 1985), two new ICMP packet types, *Address Mask Request* and *Address Mask Reply*, are proposed for the determination of the subnetwork ID address mask (see section 'Addressing at the IP level' on page 23). They have not been implemented on any UNIX system known of to date.

# Ethernet and IEEE 802.3

Ethernet is a LAN technology which was developed at the beginning of the seventies by the XEROX company. Version 2, which is predominantly used today, was standardized in 1978 by XEROX, Digital Equipment Corporation and Intel (DEC, Intel and Xerox, 1982). It is now one of the most widely used technologies for local area networks. At the beginning of the eighties, a more or less identical version was defined to be an international standard designated IEEE 802.3. There are other IEEE 802 standards (IEEE, 1983–1986) for the LAN token ring (IEEE 802.5) and token bus (IEEE 802.4) technologies.

## Connection characteristics

Ethernet is based on a coaxial cable as a bus, which is operated with a bit transmission rate of 10 million bits per second (a thousand times faster than a 9600 baud circuit). A cable segment may be up to 500 metres long and may carry up to 200 interface points (so-called *transceivers*). This version of the IEEE 802.3 standard is also known as *10Base5*. There must be a distance of at least 2.5 metres between individual transceivers. Several Ethernet cables may be connected together through so-called *repeaters* or signal amplifiers, where no more than two repeaters may be inserted between two transceivers. Thus, the maximum length of all segments is restricted to a few kilometres. Moreover, there now exist repeaters with several ports and so-called *MAC layer bridges*, which make far larger networks possible (see Chapter 7). In addition, *fan-out units* or interface multipliers are available; these may be used for simultaneous connection of several hosts per transceiver.

Thin Ethernet (*Cheapernet*) is a variant of Ethernet which differs only in its electrical connection characteristics, and not in the data transmission protocol. This variant is known as *10Base2*. The use of a thinner, more flexible cable simplifies installation and connection, in that the computer is connected directly to the cable via a transceiver integrated on the Ethernet controller card. Thus, the costs of the transceiver fall. Although the maximum cable segment length and the number of connectable stations are less than half that of Ethernet, this is no problem for small networks.    Moreover, due to the mechanical characteristics of the cable, Thin Ethernet may also be installed by non-professionals. Because Ethernet and Cheapernet are identical from the point of view of transmission speed and protocols, networks of both types may be appropriately connected via a repeater without problems.

Ethernet based on two-wire circuits (also known as *Twisted-Pair-Ethernet* or *10BaseT*) is increasingly popular. Distances of up to 30 metres between the connected stations and a junction box may be bridged using the two-wire circuits. The stations are arranged in a star shape around each junction box.

## Protocol

Ethernet uses the *Carrier Sense Multiple Access with Collision Detect* (CSMA/CD) protocol. In simple terms: before a station sends a packet, it checks to see if any other station is already active (carrier sense).    If yes, it waits until the cable is free, otherwise it transmits immediately. Should two or more stations begin by chance to transmit at the same time (collision), they recognize this situation, since they always compare the data sent with the data on the cable.    If the data is corrupted, the transmission procedure is immediately interrupted and repeated after a brief waiting time.    The waiting time is determined by a random number generator which, on retransmission, returns exponentially increasing delay values. This prevents two stations using the same waiting time forever.

The addressing uses a 48-bit address which is fixed in the hardware of every Ethernet controller.    Since the IEEE distributes numbers to the manufacturers of Ethernet controllers, it is certain that every station worldwide has a unique address.

The structure of an Ethernet packet is shown in Figure 3.18.    By way of illustration, the position of the IP and TCP protocol headers in this packet are shown; thus, the individual protocol layers may be clearly identified.

The preamble to an Ethernet packet is a special bit pattern which serves to synchronize the receiving station.    This is followed by the destination and source addresses.    In the Ethernet standard, the address of the next highest protocol is entered (in our case, this is usually IP) in the packet-type field.    Thus, various protocol layers above Ethernet may be simultaneously supported. In the IEEE 802.3 standard, the packet-type field is used as a length field; addressing of the higher level is carried out in the data section. (More of this later in the section about addressing the network layer.) After the data section of up to 1500 bits comes a 32-bit CRC checksum. Note that for technical reasons associated with transmission, a packet must be at least 64 bits long. If less data is to be sent, the packet is

**Figure 3.18**   Structure of an Ethernet packet with TCP/IP.

artificially made up to this length by the Ethernet driver in the operating system.

Each station reads the packets on the bus cable and compares the destination address with its own. If the two are the same, the station is the destination and it receives the packet completely. Because of this property (all stations in the network read each packet), a message may be simultaneously sent to all stations (*broadcast*) or to a group of stations (*multicast*). Later we shall see how broadcasts are used in a protocol to be described.

Ethernet is often criticized because of the possibility of collisions, which however are infrequent in practice because of the high transmission rate and the carrier sense procedure. Tests have shown that the number of collisions shows an above-average increase when the theoretical transmission bandwidth is loaded at the 40% level and over with packets of various lengths. According to the predominant length of the packets in the network, the load may be significantly smaller or larger (up to 90% for packets of maximum length).

## Addressing the network layer

In order to address the network layer, the Ethernet protocol header must contain an address entry. For IP, RFC 894 (Hornig, 1984) specifies entry of the value $800_{(16)}$ in the type field of the Ethernet packet.

The Ethernet 802 standard prescribes the use of the *Logical Link Control* (LLC) protocol on networks of the 802 family. The LLC protocol header contains the address of the next highest protocol. In fact, LLC has not penetrated the UNIX world and all current implementations use the mode specified in RFC 894. When, however, a host is required to use both ISO protocols (with LLC) and TCP/IP simultaneously, it must be able to determine the type of a packet on hand. Luckily, packet-type numbers specified in the RFC are longer than the maximum length of an Ethernet packet; thus, we may assume that for values up to 1500 an LLC packet is on hand.

An extended LLC protocol, the *Subnetwork Access Protocol* (SNAP) for 802 networks was proposed in RFC 1042 (Postel and Reynolds, 1988). But for Ethernets and IEEE 802.3 networks, RFC 894 is the *de facto* standard as before.

## Trailer encapsulation

*Trailer encapsulation* is a special way of sending packets in the link layer. Here, a special packet type is generated in which the IP, UDP and TCP protocol headers follow the data. In this way, the computer's receive buffer can be allocated in such a way that the data begins at a page or segment boundary of the main memory. The data length of a trailer packet is always a multiple of 512 bytes. Thus, it is possible to move the data by altering the memory management tables of the computer without copying into other address spaces. In conjunction with Ethernet, this mechanism is only advantageous for machines with small page sizes (for example, a VAX with page size 512 bytes), since the Ethernet packet itself can only be 1500 bytes long and since moreover too much bandwidth will be lost. A functional description of the protocol is given in RFC 893 (Leffler and Karels, 1984).

Ethernet trailer packets contain the values $1001_{(16)}$ or $1002_{(16)}$ in the Ethernet packet-type field, where the last position indicates the number of 512-byte blocks in the data part ($1002 = 2 * 512 = 1024$ bytes). The data is followed by the trailer of the same packet type $(800_{(16)})$, a 16-bit length field for the subsequent TCP/IP protocol headers and the TCP/IP protocol headers themselves.

In 4.2BSD, trailer encapsulation was active unless otherwise specified; since 4.3BSD, this form is on a per system basis agreed during the exchange of ARP (see later). In most UNIX systems, trailer encapsulation is no longer used today, although it is still supported on the receive side. When 4.2BSD systems are used in the network, care should be taken to ensure that either all other systems support trailer encapsulation or that they do not activate it in the first place (see *ifconfig*). Care is particularly advised in the case of non-UNIX systems, for example, Internet routers.

## ARP and RARP

As outlined in the previous sections, Ethernet, like many other subnetworks, does not use Internet addresses but its own system. Worse still, Ethernet addresses with their 48 bits are longer than Internet addresses (32 bits) and so direct association is impossible. How then, when an IP packet is sent, is the Internet address converted into a subnetwork address? There are three basic possibilities:

(1) Statistical conversion using a table. This has the disadvantage that when alterations occur in the network a new table must be generated.

(2) Conversion of Internet addresses into subnetwork addresses using a formula. For example, a station with the Ethernet address 80-04-00-60-00-01 is allocated the Internet address 89.60.00.01, where part of the Ethernet address is used for the Internet address. However, it is possible that such a conversion may not be a one-to-one correspondence; for example, if the two Ethernet addresses coincide in the fields used for conversion then both hosts will have the same Internet address.

(3) Dynamic conversions, involving interrogation in the subnetwork. In this way, for example, alterations in the Ethernet address become transparent in the network.

The third possibility may only be meaningfully implemented on a LAN with broadcast. The *Address Resolution Protocol* (ARP) was designed for this purpose and is used for the interrogation. ARP was specified in RFC 826 (Plummer, 1982) and is now supported in all Ethernet-based products.

The hardware, protocol and operation fields in Figure 3.19 specify the type of the hardware address, the software address (IP here) and the message type (question or answer).

| 0 | 7 | 15 | 31 |
|---|---|---|---|

| Hardware | Protocol |
|---|---|
| Length of HW address / Protocol length | Operation |
| Source HW address (bytes 0–3) | |
| Source HW address (bytes 4–5) | Source IP address (bytes 0–1) |
| Source IP address (bytes 2–3) | Destination HW address (bytes 0–1) |
| Destination HW address (bytes 2–5) | |
| Destination IP address (bytes 0–3) | |

**Figure 3.19**  ARP protocol header.

The functional description of ARP is as follows:

(1) IP presents a datagram at the Ethernet network interface of computer A, which searches for the corresponding Ethernet address in its own (temporary) table. If there is a valid entry, an Ethernet packet with this address is provided and sent.

(2) If there is no valid entry, an ARP broadcast packet with the Internet address of the target host is generated and sent.

(3) All computers in the network receive the ARP packet and compare the Internet address it contains with their own. The computer (B) with the same address sends an ARP response containing the desired Ethernet address back to computer A.

(4) Computer A enters the address from computer B in its table and sends the IP packet and the subsequent IP packets direct to computer B.

To make the association more dynamic, the entries in the temporary table are deleted after a certain time (1 to 20 minutes, depending on the implementation) and the interrogation is repeated. Since a search procedure only takes a few milliseconds, this process is practically transparent.

RARP stands for *Reverse* ARP and is used in the opposite case, to determine an Internet address, for example, by a diskless workstation during the load operation over the network. Such workstations require their own Internet addresses in order to communicate with a TFTP daemon. (The Ethernet address usually comes from the memory of the station's own Ethernet controller.) RARP is specified in RFC 903 (Finlayson *et al.*, 1984). Recently, this mechanism has been replaced by *BOOTP*, described in RFC 951 (Croft and Gilmore, 1985). The latter uses a much simpler mechanism for initiating the load operation of diskless workstations based on IP datagrams.

RARP uses the same packet format as ARP, but with different operation codes. RARP enquiries are also sent using network broadcast. One of the computers must have an active RARP server which responds to enquiries using a table containing the Internet address corresponding to the Ethernet address. In order to operate an RARP server, direct access to the Ethernet layer from a user program is required; this is not implemented in all UNIX systems.

# Serial Line IP

4.3BSD included an implementation of the *Serial Line Interface Protocol* (SLIP). SLIP permits the connection of two computers over a serial line (for example, V.24). SLIP is a very simple protocol and was later specified in RFC 1055 (Romkey, 1988).

All SLIP packets begin with a byte with value $EB_{(16)}$ in the protocol known as ESC. The data is followed by a $C0_{(16)}$ (END). If these values occur in the data, they are sent as a 2-byte sequence ESC $EC_{(16)}$ or ESC $ED_{(16)}$ and reconverted into END or ESC by the recipient. No maximum packet length is prescribed, since by convention the expected upper bound is 1006 bytes.

SLIP does not contain addresses or other protocol fields and only serves to format the data into packets for transporting over a point-to-point connection. Any UNIX machine may be easily converted into a gateway (for example, to connect two Ethernets across building boundaries) using the SLIP driver delivered with most UNIX implementations and a serial line. However, for transmission rates of (usually) at most 19200 bauds, there is a marked drop in performance in comparison with the Ethernet operation, to say nothing of the possible overloading of the UNIX processor due to the use of the serial line.

As a countermeasure, a protocol has been proposed in RFC 1144 (Jacobson, 1990) which decreases the packet size on SLIP links by compressing the TCP/IP protocol header. The algorithm is based on the fact that most of the information in the TCP/IP protocol header does not change during the lifetime of a connection (Internet addresses, port numbers, etc.). Using a private connection identifier, both sides only send the header fields which have actually changed since the last packet exchange. The benefits are actually overwhelming: the average TCP/IP protocol header is reduced from 40 to 3 bytes for most cases. Since the most used applications in the network are remote login or TELNET, which usually only send a character at a time, the ratio of user to protocol data in a packet is improved through compression by a factor of 10. Implementations of this, as yet non-standard, protocol are in use at various sites; however, they are not widely available from UNIX vendors.

## X.25

In recent years, X.25 has become increasingly popular as a means of building wide area TCP/IP networks. Support for X.25 comes in two flavours: either as a self-contained Internet router which is connected to the network or as a UNIX subnetwork interface driver, turning the UNIX system into a gateway. The latter is less common due to the lack of reference implementations. In both cases, an X.25 connection is used as a direct link between two systems, very much like a SLIP link.

However, X.25 connections are not usually established statically, but created dynamically, depending on the Internet addresses of the packets arriving at the subnetwork interface. If the X.25 connection is not used for some time, it may be severed temporarily with any still active TCP connections remaining unaffected.

A standard described in RFC 877 (Korb, 1983) specifies a way of transmitting IP datagrams over X.25. The most interesting feature of RFC 877 is that it specifies IP datagrams to be sent as complete packet sequences; that is, datagrams larger than a maximum size X.25 packet should not be fragmented by IP, but sent as multiple X.25 packets linked by the 'M' bit in the X.25 protocol header. Thus, the overhead of an additional IP protocol header per X.25 packet is saved; fragmentation and reassembly of the IP datagram is handled in the X.25 interface driver.

# TCP/IP – layers 5 to 7

- TELNET

- File Transfer Protocol

- Simple Mail Transfer Protocol

- Trivial File Transfer Protocol

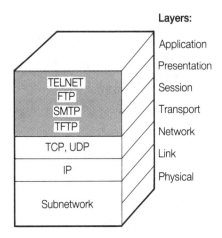

**Figure 4.1** The higher protocol layers of the TCP/IP architecture.

In the previous chapter, we were concerned with the protocols of the lower layers. However, as mentioned in the introductory chapter, the TCP/IP architecture also has a set of standardized application protocols (Figure 4.1). Even though these have recently been replaced in part by more modern services and applications, more in correspondence with the increased requirements in modern computing, it is still worth learning more about them. In what follows, we shall consider the protocols together with the corresponding UNIX commands.

## TELNET

TELNET is specified in RFC 854 (Postel and Reynolds, 1983). It is intended to provide access, in the form of a terminal session (also called *remote login* or *virtual terminal*), to a computer connected to the network. In UNIX systems, the *telnet* command is used on the client side, while on the server side (the computer called over *telnet*) there is a so-called daemon or server known as *telnetd*. The TELNET service is attached to TCP port 23.

UNIX processors currently incorporate the *rlogin* command, which offers almost the same functionality as *telnet* but provides better support for the UNIX environment. In fact, the TELNET protocol contains elements which, in particular, support joint working with large computer systems; thus, it is preferred for heterogeneous operation. (We shall return to *rlogin* in detail later.)

## A telnet session

*telnet* is usually called with a computer name. A port number may also be entered: this allows for the manual execution of a dialogue with other services (for example, SMTP). If no computer name is given, *telnet* goes into command mode and issues a prompt. In the command mode, connections to computers may be created and cancelled, the operating parameters may be modified and much more. An escape character (usually ^], given by simultaneously pressing the keys ctrl and ]) may be used at any time to change to this mode. In the case of an active connection, *telnet* returns to the network connection after each command.

On activation of *telnet*, a TCP connection to the target computer and to *telnetd* (whence to the server) is set up. *telnetd* then organizes the remainder of the procedure so that the login process to which one is usually accustomed on a local terminal proceeds over the newly created connection (over an 'artificial' terminal so to speak). The result is a window into the server computer, where there runs a shell in which programs may be activated as usual.

After this, in UNIX systems, every input or output character passes through three different processes (in both directions), as shown in Figure 4.2:

- the *telnet* command at the terminal;
- the *telnetd* server which handles the TELNET protocol on the server side;
- the application program, which is started by the server computer over this connection;
- and all the way back to the terminal.

Certain UNIX programs, such as editors, operate only in conjunction with terminals and use modes which may only be selected in the terminal driver. Thus, applications and the *telnetd* process are connected via a so-called pseudo terminal driver. To the application program, the pseudo terminal looks like an interface to a normal terminal. *telnetd* sits at the point where the terminal hardware is connected, where it accepts outputs from the applications and forwards them to the *telnet* user program in

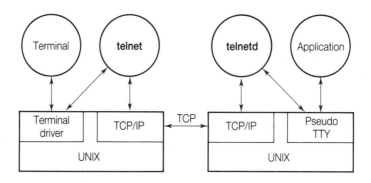

**Figure 4.2**   Schematic diagram of a TELNET session under UNIX.

the other computer. The pseudo terminal driver acts like a normal terminal driver: it processes control characters, generates echoes for all characters entered, etc.

## Mode of operation of the TELNET protocol

It is well known that the operation of computer systems and the capabilities of the terminals connected to them vary greatly from system to system. This area has been to some extent standardized for the user by the introduction of standard operating systems such as UNIX, MS-DOS and OS/2. A protocol which is required to operate between arbitrary systems in the very heterogeneous data-processing world must either be restricted as far as its permissible functions are concerned or very flexible in its ability to adapt to any encountered behaviour.

A middle road was selected in the TELNET protocol: this involves a small number of message-format specifications and anything else is negotiated between the two partners in the session.

## Network virtual terminal

TELNET defines a so-called *Network Virtual Terminal* (NVT) to describe the capabilities of the data sources and destinations. The NVT consists of a virtual keyboard which generates only specific characters and a virtual printer which can only display specific characters. This determines the

**Figure 4.3**  Schematic diagram of a network virtual terminal.

functional scope of the input and output sides. Every end point of a TELNET connection logically consists of an NVT keyboard and an NVT printer, as shown schematically in Figure 4.3. Precise details are given in the TELNET specification. The NVT is, as it were, a specification of the presentation layer and is thus of major importance. Outside TELNET, the NVT format is also used in the FTP and SMTP protocols.

## TELNET options

Both parties to a TELNET connection provide services which may be switched on and off by TELNET protocol elements known as options. At the beginning of the TELNET session, client and server negotiate the modes to be set. However, options may also be negotiated at any time during the active session. In UNIX machines, the TELNET server and client set modes which correspond to the mode of operation of the UNIX terminal: transfer of the terminal designation and character-serial input with echo through the TELNET server. Other settings may be preferred on large computers.

The transaction continues using four special protocol verbs: *do, don't, will* and *won't.* Here, *do* and *will* are requests or offers to the communication partner to provide a certain service, and *don't* and *won't* are the opposite. Semantically, these protocol codes are defined in such

```
$ telnet
telnet> toggle options
Will show option processing.
telnet> open train1
Trying...
Connected to train1.
Escape character is '^]'.
SENT do SUPPRESS GO AHEAD
SENT will TERMINAL TYPE (reply)
RCVD do TERMINAL TYPE (don't reply)
RCVD will SUPPRESS GO AHEAD (don't reply)
RCVD will ECHO (reply)
SENT do ECHO (reply)
RCVD do ECHO (reply)
SENT wont ECHO (reply)

System V UNIX (train1)

RCVD dont ECHO (don't reply)
login: test
Password:
UNIX System V/386 Release 3.2 i386
train1
Copyright (c) 1987 AT&T
All Rights Reserved
$ date
Sat Jun 10 19:17:34 GMT 1989
$ ^]
telnet> quit
Connection closed by foreign host.
$
```

**Figure 4.4**   *telnet* dialogue with option handling and explicit interruption.

a way that requests and offers for the same output act as answers to one
another. Figure 4.4 shows the transaction of TELNET options between two
UNIX systems using internal commands in the *telnet* program. Note how
the change from the input mode to the command mode takes place and how
the session is explicitly broken off.

# File Transfer Protocol

The *File Transfer Protocol* (FTP) is specified in RFC 959 (Postel and Reynolds, 1985). TCP port 21 is fixed as the command channel and TCP port 20 as the data channel. In UNIX systems, the protocol is the command of the same name *ftp* and the server is *ftpd*.

FTP differs from other file transfer programs in many respects. The most prominent differences include the use of separate channels for control information and data and the fact that FTP data transfers do not run in the background (work without a spooler).

As protocol elements, FTP uses ASCII text in the NVT format, terminated by a new-line symbol, consisting of a four-character command word with optional parameters. Return codes contain a three-figure digital code and an accompanying text which explains the success or failure of the action. Codes beginning with the numbers 1, 2 or 3 are positive return codes, while codes 4 or 5 stand for errors. The subsequent numbers give a more detailed description of the return code and the error. The fact that the protocol elements are coded in ASCII simplifies debugging and it is also possible to communicate interactively with the FTP server. The FTP protocol commands may be used to send, receive, delete and rename files, to create, delete and change directories, to send electronic mail, to append to files and much more.

For every data transfer, a TCP connection between client and server is opened, which is closed again after transmission. In this way, FTP uses the reliability features of TCP and, since all necessary precautionary measures for error-free transmission are already in hand, it does not need to use any reliability features of its own.

Although many transmission modes (for example, data compression) are specified, only two modes are implemented on UNIX systems, namely, the text mode and the binary mode. In the text mode, text files are sent as ASCII lines separated by carriage return and new-line symbols; in this way, they can be transferred between two different types of system. In binary mode, a file is transmitted, without conversion, as a sequence of bytes, which is naturally a good deal faster. At the start, text mode is initially set. For transmissions between two similar systems (for example, UNIX systems), for reasons of speed, binary mode should also be used for text files.

## ftp command

At the beginning of an FTP session, a connection to the server FTP must be set up. This is done by supplying the computer name with the *ftp* command, or using the *open* command in the FTP command mode, as for *telnet*. To execute a file transfer, it is necessary to obtain access rights to the file. This is done by logging on to the server computer, giving a login name and a password. After the login, one remains logically, on the client computer, as before, and not on the server computer, as in TELNET. This should be noted when commands are executed.

Now one of the many FTP commands may be activated. In the example in Figure 4.5, the debug option has been switched on to show the exchanges which occur in the command channel. As can be seen, the execution of a session is very easy to follow. Arrows indicate a message from the client; lines with three figures at the beginning denote replies from the server. Regrettably, data transfer cannot be followed in this way. The *quote* command may be used to enter FTP protocol messages directly. The HELP command provides, for example, a list of the FTP protocol elements implemented in the server. PORT calls signal the address of a data channel on which the client is waiting to the server. If the PORT call is missing, TCP port 20 is used as standard.

The following *ftp* commands are used very frequently:

| *ftp command* | *Explanation* |
|---|---|
| *get* | Fetch a file from the server. |
| *put* | Send a file to the server. |
| *del* | Delete a file in the server. |
| *binary* | Switch into binary transmission mode. |
| *cd* | Change the directory on the server. |
| *lcd* | Change the directory on the client. |
| *pwd* | Display the contents of a name on the server. |
| *dir* | Display the directory on the server. |
| *hash* | Display a # character for each transmitted block. |
| *quit* | End the *ftp* command. |

In addition, there are many other commands which are intended to facilitate work with *ftp*. Automation using a command file with the name *.netrc* in one's own Login directory is also possible. This may be used to construct a range of computer-specific command macros. As for *telnet*, you should run through some of the *ftp* commands from the handbook yourself at the terminal, so you can better appreciate the capabilities of this program.

One disadvantage of *ftp* is that the program cannot transfer the access rights from the source file to the target file (this is not technically provided for in the protocol). Furthermore, file trees may not be transmitted.

```
$ ftp -d
ftp> open train2
Connected to train2.
220 train2 FTP server (Version 4.4 Tue Dec 20 1988) ready.
Name (train2:kurs1): kurs1
331 Password required for kurs1.
Password:  ...
230 User kurs1 logged in.
ftp> dir
--> PORT 192,9,150,244,4,57
200 PORT command successful.
--> LIST
150 Opening data connection for /bin/ls -1 (...
total 1
-rw ------- 1 kurs1   ixos   240 May 18 10:53 test
226 Transfer complete.
100 bytes received in 1 second (0.66 kbyte/s)
ftp> get test
--> PORT 192,9,150,244,4,59
200 PORT command successful.
--> RETR test
150 Opening data connection for test (192.9.150.244,1083)
226 Transfer complete.
local: test remote: test
250 bytes received in 0 second (0.24 kbyte/s)
ftp> quote HELP
--> HELP
214-These commands are recognized (*'s unimplemented)
USER     PORT     RETR     MSND*    ALLO     DELE
SITE*    XMKD     CDUP     PASS     PASV     STOR
MSOM*    REST*    CWD      STAT*    RMD      XCUP
ACCT*    TYPE     APPE     MSAM*    RNFR     XCWD
HELP     XRMD     STOU     REIN*    STRU     MLFL*
MRSQ*    RNTO     LIST     NOOP     PWD      SYST
QUIT     MODE     MAIL*    MRCP*    ABOR     NLST
MKD      XPWD
214 Direct comments to ftp-bugs@train2.
ftp> quit
--> QUIT
221 Goodbye.
```

**Figure 4.5**   Outputs of an FTP session.

## Simple Mail Transfer Protocol

The *Simple Mail Transfer Protocol* (SMTP) is the Internet protocol for electronic mail specified in RFC 821 (Postel, 1982). TCP port 25 is defined for SMTP. Like TELNET and FTP, SMTP is distinguished by its simplicity; it incorporates many features of FTP.

As can be seen from the sample dialogue in Figure 4.6, a mail transfer can be accomplished with remarkably few protocol elements:

| Command | Explanation |
|---------|-------------|
| HELO | Introduction of the client to the server. |
| MAIL | Declaration of the sender's address. Replies, error messages, etc. will be sent to this address. |
| RCPT | Declaration of the message destination. There may be several consecutive RCPT commands, so that data may be sent to several destinations but transmitted only once. |
| DATA | Message text in ASCII format (7 bits). The end of the message is indicated by a single full stop at the beginning of a line. If a line of the message begins with a full stop, the sender SMTP adds another full stop, which will be removed by the other party. If the destination SMTP replies with a positive acknowledgement, the message was successfully received. |
| QUIT | End of the SMTP dialogue. |

```
220 balahe.ixos.de Sendmail 5.1 ready at Sat, 10 Jun ...
HELO mitsouko.ixos.de
250 balahe.ixos.de Hello mitsouko.ixos.de, pleased ...
MAIL From:<santi@mitsouko>
250 <santi@mitsouko>...  Sender ok
RCPT To:roland
250 roland...  Recipient ok
DATA
354 Enter mail, end with "." on a line by itself
Date: 10 Jun 89 11:22:33
From: <santi@mitsouko.ixos.de>
To: <roland@balahe.ixos.de>
Subject: All OK

Mitsouko is active again as of now.
.
250 Ok
QUIT
221 balahe.ixos.de closing connection
```

**Figure 4.6** SMTP dialogue.

The three-figure codes of FTP are used for replies and acknowledgements. Address entry follows the conventions of the *Domain Name System* (DNS), which we shall discuss in Chapter 7 on internetworking.

Other SMTP protocol elements are:

| Command | Explanation |
|---------|-------------|
| VRFY | Verification of a user name. The recipient attempts to return the full name of the user and the address of his mailbox in reply. |
| EXPN | Expansion of distribution lists. The recipient provides a list of the people with names and mailbox addresses. |
| SEND | Send a message to a user's terminal. In addition to SEND, there are also SOML (Send or Mail) and SAML (Send and Mail). |
| TURN | Change the send direction. The current recipient becomes the message sender. |
| RSET | Termination of the current mail transaction. |
| HELP | Request for help information. |
| NOOP | No operation. |

## sendmail

In UNIX systems, SMTP is implemented by the program */usr/lib/sendmail*. This is a very complex program which is able to communicate with mail services other than SMTP and which to some extent also operates as a gateway between different mail systems.

*sendmail* may function not only as SMTP server, but also as SMTP client. However, the user never uses *sendmail* directly, but usually through a so-called *front end*, such as *mailx*, which controls and simplifies the entry of the message. *sendmail* is only activated to forward the message. If forwarding is not immediately possible, the message is entered into an output queue in the directory */usr/spool/mqueue*. Regular attempts are then made to forward the message from there to the destination. The job queue may be inspected by the program *mailq*, which is a link to *sendmail*.

On the server side, *sendmail* is activated on system start together with other servers on the computer; it then waits for incoming TCP connection requests. This server process also takes charge of the repeated forwarding from the queue.

*sendmail* is controlled by means of a configuration file (*/usr/lib/sendmail.cf*) which makes the program very adaptable. In addition to the definition of the local mail-forwarding program and many other things, this file also contains the commands for converting the address for the connected mail system. A great many system managers have already been reduced to tears through attempts to understand the syntax and content of conversion rules and many other options. Usually, *sendmail* is supplied with an operable configuration file, which need not be modified other than for local adjustments.

It is also worth mentioning the alias file, which is built into *sendmail* and which the network administrator may use to create distribution lists and forwarding requests. The alias file in */usr/lib/aliases* is edited by the network administrator and is then converted into an indexed database using the *newaliases* command. Like *mailq*, *newaliases* is a link to *sendmail*. Alias names may also be used to send messages to programs, for example, to set up an automatic answering service.

It is practical to install a mail-distribution computer, to which all mail is initially sent and which then forwards the message to the private mailbox of the recipient. In this way, mail addresses only need to be held and managed on the mail-distribution computer, which can greatly ease the administration of the mail service. Another way of doing this is to use the DNS which also handles mailbox addresses. A user may also initiate the forwarding of mail himself by creating a file with the name *.forward* in his Login directory. The message is then immediately forwarded to the forwarding address contained in this file, without detours over a local service.

## Trivial File Transfer Protocol

The *Trivial File Transfer Protocol* (TFTP) is a file transfer protocol with minimal requirements. It is specified in RFC 783 (Sollins, 1981) and uses UDP port 69.

Like FTP, TFTP also supports a text and a binary transmission mode. The main difference from FTP is the use of a connectionless transport protocol, UDP in our case. This has several consequences as far as the structure of the protocol is concerned. Firstly, TFTP must itself be responsible for transmission reliability via algorithms such as time monitoring and packet retransmission. Moreover, the process does not involve logging on to the server computer; the TFTP server replaces this lack of authorization by restrictive access constraints, so that, for example, on UNIX processors, files may only be read and written to if their access rights make them available to be read and written by all users. The protocol specification does not prescribe how a system should protect itself against illegal access over TFTP, so this is therefore implementation specific.

The TFTP protocol codes are:

- Read Request (RRQ)
- Write Request (WRQ)
- Send Data (DATA)

- Acknowledgement (ACK)
- Error (ERROR).

Communication between the TFTP server and the client begins with RRQ or WRQ packets. In this way, transaction IDs are exchanged which are later used to identify the data packets. They also contain the file names and an entry regarding the transmission mode to be used. DATA packets are used to transmit the actual data and the server receives an ACK or an ERROR packet in reply. The transmission is deemed to be closed when a DATA packet of length less than 512 bytes is received.

It is not difficult to see that TFTP can have no advantages as far as regular file transfer between systems is concerned. While TFTP is used for such purposes in exceptional cases, this protocol is currently mainly used in loading server programs and fonts in X window terminals and in bootstrapping diskless workstations. In the latter case, TFTP is used to transfer the system program into the main memory (see RFC 906 (Finlayson, 1984)). This is because of the low operational requirements of TFTP: in addition to the protocol itself, only the IP base functions, the very simple UDP protocol and a driver to access the network, are required. Such a protocol may be implemented very cheaply and the result stored in a few kilobytes of memory, for example, on an EPROM.

```
$ tftp
tftp> connect train2

tftp> binary

tftp> trace
Packet tracing on.
tftp> verbose
Verbose mode on.
tftp> get /usr1/kurs1/test /tmp/test
getting from train2:/usr1/kurs1/test to /tmp/test [octet]
sent RRQ <file=/usr1/kurs1/test, mode=octet>
received DATA <block=1, 512 bytes>
sent ACK <block=1>
received DATA <block=4, 373 bytes>
Received 885 bytes in 0.1 second [50907 bits/s]
tftp> status
Connected to train2.
Mode:  octet Verbose: on Tracing: on
Rexmt-interval: 5 seconds, Max-timeout: 25 seconds
tftp> quit
$
```

**Figure 4.7**  Outputs of a TFTP session.

### tftp

As usual, UNIX systems contain a *tftp* command corresponding to the
TFTP protocol of the same name. The corresponding server is called
*tftpd*. The options available and the operation of *tftp* are very similar to
the *ftp* command, but less comprehensive (for example, the authorization
process is missing). The user should note the access constraints referred
to earlier. Figure 4.7 shows a sample *tftp* dialogue on a UNIX system.
Here, the *connect* command does not establish a connection but determines
the partner address for subsequent actions. *verbose* and *trace* make the
exchange of the protocol elements visible.

# 5

# Berkeley r-utilities

- *$HOME/.rhosts* and */etc/hosts.equiv*
- *rlogin*
- *rsh*
- *rcp*
- *ruptime* and *rwho*
- *rexec*

The integration of TCP/IP into UNIX by the University of California in Berkeley was a decisive contribution to the success of the TCP/IP architecture. The developers in Berkeley did not restrict themselves to the implementation of existing protocols and services such as FTP and TELNET, but also developed their own, sometimes very UNIX-specific, commands. The commands are the consequent conversion of existing UNIX commands into a networked environment; thus, today in an 'open' UNIX environment, the Berkeley r-utilities are used almost exclusively. They are termed r-utilities because they begin with the letter *r*, as in *remote*. In addition to the r-utilities, a full range of commands (not discussed in detail here) has been developed over the years. This chapter is concerned with the attributes of the r-utilities.

## $HOME/.rhosts and /etc/hosts.equiv

In addition to their particular suitability for UNIX systems, some of the Berkeley utilities have another special attribute: the equating of login names over computer boundaries. Correctly configured, this eliminates the tedious typing in of login names and passwords on accessing other computers in the network; access now follows without further checks. The relevant commands are *rlogin*, *rsh* and *rcp*. Moreover, all commands are TCP based.

The mechanism for equating network-wide login names is very simple and therefore insufficient for systems with security requirements. The greatest weakness is, as in many other instances in UNIX systems, the status of the *super-user*. If a potential penetrator knows the super-user password for just one computer in the network, he may, having the necessary knowledge, penetrate all the other computers. In practice, the mechanism used by the r-utilities has provided adequate protection, since, while there are people who know a super-user password, none of them has the necessary knowledge or criminal energy to take advantage of this.

The mode of operation is as follows: the server computer contains tables which specify the pairs of client and server login names which may work together. The client login name is transmitted immediately after connection set-up in the form of an ASCII character string. Server programs protect themselves from misuse in that they only trust the client's login name entry when the TCP connection on the client side comes from a region of privileged TCP ports (ports 1 to 1023). These ports may only be accessed by the super-user. Thus, all commands which use this authorization scheme have the Setuser-ID bit set and belong to the login name *root*. The function of the privileged ports, which exist in both TCP and UDP, is purely UNIX specific; thus, these ports may be freely accessed in every other operating system. Moreover, this concept avoids passwords being transmitted in clear (when they might be intercepted) within the network.

```
$ hostname
aramis
$ id
uid=2015(santi) gid=100
$ cat $HOME/.rhosts
aramis santi
loopback santi
mitsouko santi
joop root
ixos santi
ixos roland
$
```

**Figure 5.1**   Example of a .rhosts file.

Access rights are controlled on the server computer by a configuration
file which may be system wide or user specific.    An individual user
may use the file .rhosts in his Login directory to allow other users on
other computers to use his login name. On the other hand, the network
administrator may declare all login names of another computer whose host
name is entered in the file /etc/hosts.equiv to be equivalent; in this
case, nominally identical login names have the same basic access. On most
systems, for understandable reasons, the login name root is excluded from
this; it can only be made accessible by specific permission in the .rhosts
file of the super-user.

Files are searched for authorizing entries, firstly system wide then
user specifically; the .rhosts file is only searched if no suitable entry is
found in /etc/hosts.equiv. The .rhosts file must belong to the given
login name or to root and must not be available for universal write access;
this prevents the use of a 'Trojan horse'.

An entry in the .rhosts file consists of a computer name and a
login name. The .rhosts file shown in Figure 5.1 permits the login name
santi of computers aramis, loopback, mitsouko and ixos, the login
name roland of computer ixos and the login name root of computer joop
to access the login name santi on computer aramis. The inclusion of the
original local login name in this list may be surprising, but in practice local
access to one's own login name is commonly required for test purposes (for
example, to check the functional integrity of the local TCP/IP system).
The same effect would be obtained by entering the name of the original
computer in /etc/hosts.equiv for all local login names.

# rlogin

The name *rlogin* stands for *remote login*; thus, this command allows one to login on a different computer. The corresponding server is *rlogind*, which waits for connection requests on TCP port 513. As in *telnet*, so too here, a login procedure is initiated in the server computer and a pseudo terminal is set up. There are very few functional differences from *telnet* on UNIX systems.

The *rlogin* protocol is very simple. At the beginning of the session, three character strings ('[1]...[3]'), separated by zeros, are sent:

[1]   This contains the original login name in the client computer, namely, the ID under which the *rlogin* was initiated.

[2]   This contains the login name in the server computer which it is desired to sign on to. As a standard, the same name is entered here as in the first character string; any other name may be entered using the option *- l*. If corresponding entries exist on the server computer, an automatic login takes place, otherwise a password and/or a login name must be explicitly given.

[3]   This contains the login name and the transmission rate of the terminal at which the user is working on the client computer (for example, *vt100/9600*). The terminal ID is transferred in the server to the TERM variable, so that applications started there send the appropriate terminal control characters. The connection speed is stored as information within the internal structure of the pseudo terminal so that waiting times for terminal control characters may be correctly calculated.

*rlogin* does not use any other protocol; all characters entered at the keyboard are transparently sent to the server and all characters issued there are displayed on the user screen of the client computer.

As a rule, *rlogin* is terminated by termination of the local shell, for example, by entering ^D. If this control character has no effect (possibly because of a 'hanging program'), an explicit termination may be produced by entering ~. at the beginning of the line. The escape character ~ may be arbitrarily redefined using the *- e* option. In some systems, by entering ~!, it is possible to branch temporarily into a local shell or (if there is more text after the exclamation mark) to execute a local command.

It is possible to associate the *rlogin* program file with the name of a server computer. Thus, it is possible to initiate a session simply by entering the name of a computer.

---

                    *... Normal command ...*
$ *rsh aramis date*
Wed Nov 22 23:50:16 GMT 1989

                    *... Transfer of data from server ...*
$ *rsh mitsouko cat /etc/passwd | grep santi*
santi:x:2015:100:Michael Santifaller:/usr/santi:

                    *... Initiation of commands with local data ...*
$ *rsh joop —l reinhard lp <printfile*

                    *... Data back-up on server computer ...*
$ *tar cvfb — 20 fred.c | rsh ixos dd of=/dev/rmt0 bs=20b*
a fred 657 tape blocks
$ *rsh ixos dd if=/dev/rmt0 bs=20b | tar tvfb — 20*
tar:  blocksize = 20
r—r—r—2015/100 336120 Nov 22 22:42 1989 fred

                    *... Pipelining of commands via several computers ...*
$ *tbl —D text | rsh aramis troff —mm | lp*

                    *... Copying by suppression of Shell meta-character expansion ...*
$ *rsh aramis 'cat>fred'<santi*

---

**Figure 5.2**  Possible applications of *rsh*.

# rsh

---

The *remote shell rsh* and the corresponding server *rshd* (TCP port 514) allow the user to execute commands on a different computer. In System V, there is a 'restricted shell' of the same name as this command, but it has nothing to do with the command; in this case, the shell is sometimes available under the name *remsh* or *rcmd*.

   *rsh* is not a shell in the true sense, in that it does not interpret command calls itself. The command line entered as a parameter is sent to the server, at which time *rsh* connects the UNIX standard input and output channels *stdin, stdout* and *stderr* of the newly initiated command with the process running locally by means of two TCP connections. This means that many UNIX commands may be used without alteration. The few examples in Figure 5.2 clearly show how powerful the UNIX pipe concept may be when associated with the *rsh* command.

There are also some restrictions:

- The exit code of the command in the server computer is not returned. Thus, in shell procedures, it is not possible to check whether or not the command was successfully executed.

- Terminal-oriented programs, such as editors, either do not run under *rsh* or run only with restrictions, since they expect a terminal as input and output channel.

- Terminal names are not given, consequently programs such as *pg*, which expect this information, fail.

- The UNIX signals interrupt (SIGINT), quit (SIGQUIT) and terminate (SIGTERM), which are sent locally to the *rsh* process, should be forwarded to the sender and then sent to the process group of the command. We have however established more than once that this clearly does not work on various systems.

The command given as a parameter is interpreted in the server processor through a shell (for example, *sh  −c*); thus, shell meta-characters, such as output rerouting by '>', may also be used. On the client side, these must be enclosed by quotes to protect them from interpretation by the local shell. The Login directory is used as the current directory on the server. The shell used in the server computer is that given in */etc/passwd* with the option *−c*. If individual shells, programs or shell procedures are entered in */etc/passwd* in lieu of */bin/sh*, they must be capable of understanding the *−c* option. Shell configuration files, such as *.profile* or *.login*, are not executed; consequently, user-specific defaults for command directories and the like have no effect.

A prerequisite for operation of the *rsh* call is the presence of entries in *.rhosts* or */etc/hosts.equiv*; an interactive login is not possible.

If there is no suitable entry, the message `Permission denied` appears on the screen. Like the *rlogin* command, *rsh* also uses the original login name in the remote computer, but a different name may be entered using the option *−l*. It is also possible to shorten the call by association with a host name: *rsh* calls *rlogin* when no command line is given.

The programmer can use the services of the *rshd* process with the library routine *rcmd()* and build it into his own applications.  *rcmd()* generates the connection to the server and executes the protocols needed for authentication and for transfer of the command line.

# rcp

*rcp* is the Berkeley utilities file transfer command which operates like an extension of the *cp* command in the network.  All applications of *cp*

---

*... Normal command ...*
```
$ rcp aramis:/etc/passwd fred
$ rcp fred aramis:.
$ rcp aramis:fred sam
```
        *... Transfer between third-party computers ...*
```
$ rcp mitsouko:file1 aramis:file1
```
        *... Use of another user ID ...*
```
$ rcp sam santi@joop:test
```

---

**Figure 5.3**    Possible applications of the **rcp** command.

which may be useful in a network (for example, copying of local files from remote computers and vice versa, copying between three computers and local copying) are implemented by *rcp*. Recursive copying of whole data trees is also possible with the $-r$ option (this is a function which *ftp* does not provide, but which is very frequently required in practice). Moreover, the access rights of the source files are transferred to the target files. The $-p$ option may also be used to permit the modification time of the source file to be transferred to the target file.

    *rcp* extends the file names by adding a host name separated by a colon, as in *aramis:fred* (see Figure 5.3). Path names are interpreted according to the Login directory of the login name used in the server. Of course, absolute path names such as *aramis:/etc/passwd* may also be used. If no path name is given after the colon, the entry refers to the Login directory. For the login name in the server, the same login name is again used as standard. If this is not desired, the host name must be given with an extension, for example, *santi@aramis:test* (old systems such as 4.2BSD also use *aramis.santi:test*). It is possible to enter regular expressions in file names. Note however that these must be protected from expansion by the local shell.

    The *rcp* program may operate as client or (with the internal option $-t$) as server; thus, two *rcp* programs work together at the same time. The *rcp* server process is in this case initiated by *rsh* in the server computer. This means that, as for *rsh*, the entries in *.rhosts* etc. must be present. *rcp* does not function if the shell configuration file (for example, *.cshrc*) generates an output.

```
$ rwho
beate      shalimar:ttyp1  Jun 19 11:49
bogi       joop:tty03      Jun 19 07:07
cornelia   chloe:ttyp0     Jun 19 09:18 :05
daniel     fidji:tty00     Jun 19 09:48
elli       drakkar:tty03   Jun 19 10:32
hsz        joop:tty09      Jun 14 15:48 :03
jan        chloe:tty00     Jun 19 06:13
snoopy     joop:tty08      Jun 19 07:23
$ ruptime
chanel   down 2+15:48
chloe    up       4:49, 2 users, load 0.06, 0.05, 0.00
dior     down     0:41
drakkar  up    6+02:30, 1 user,  load 0.10, 0.01, 0.00
fidji    up    4+03:22, 2 users, load 0.12, 0.05, 0.00
halston  up       3:31, 1 user,  load 0.18, 0.13, 0.09
ixos     up   17+22:23, 0 users, load 0.00, 0.00, 0.00
joop     up    9+16:07, 5 users, load 0.42, 0.25, 0.08
$
```

**Figure 5.4**  Outputs from *rwho* and *ruptime*.

## ruptime and rwho

*ruptime* and *rwho* are services provided using the *rwhod* daemon (UDP port 513) which runs on every processor.

*ruptime* displays a list of the computers in the network, their load, the number of users signed on and the elapsed time since the last system start (Figure 5.4). The 4.2/4.3BSD program *uptime* was a prototype.

*rwho*, as the name indicates, displays a list of all users signed on to the network, as in the local *who* command (Figure 5.4). This is possible using information from the *rwhod* daemon which, on each processor, regularly sends a UDP broadcast packet containing entries about the system and its users in the network. In 4.2BSD, this happens every minute; in 4.3BSD, every three minutes. All other *rwhod*s in the network receive this packet and read it into the directory */usr/spool/rwho*. Thus, *rwhod* both generates and uses the messages.

The two commands *rwho* and *ruptime* only read the information from the files in */usr/spool/rwho* and process it. Both use the same conventions regarding the interpretation of the modification time:

- If a processor has not sent any messages for 11 minutes, it is deemed to be inactive and the users signed on there are no longer indicated.
- Users who have not entered anything at the terminal for an hour are likewise removed from the list, unless the −*a* option is given.

The method of persistent sending used by *rwhod* has a significant disadvantage: in very large networks it leads to an unnecessary loading of the network. In networks with diskless workstations, it has an even worse effect: in certain circumstances, on receipt of the packet, the program pages of all *rwhod* daemons must be fetched by the server computer and, moreover, the received packets must be stored on the server processor. Thus, there is considerable activity in the network each time a packet is sent and this activity may hinder other processes. On the other hand, the information is in general only used sporadically.

Sun Microsystems has developed another solution in which the information is only fetched when it is actually required. Sun systems therefore contain server programs called *ruserd* and *rstatd* which fetch the required information about RPC requests when needed by the commands *rusers* and *rstatus*.

## rexec

The *rexecd* daemon provides another way of initiating commands on other computers. It uses TCP port 512.

The protocol used by *rexecd* is similar to that of *rshd*, with the major difference that an encrypted password is sent with the request and thus there is normal authentication, as for a login. The *rexec* service is as a rule only obtainable via a program interface in the C library in the shape of the routine *rexec()*. Some systems also have a corresponding *rexec* command.

The *rexec* interface has not succeeded in practice since users clearly prefer the more comfortable automation of *rsh*. However, it is supported in all implementations.

# 6

# TCP/IP administration

- Loopback driver
- Configuration files in /etc
- *hostname*
- *netstat*
- *ifconfig*
- *arp*
- *ping*
- *trpt*
- *inetd*

Often, a user waits in vain for connection to another computer or a specific server. For most problems, on UNIX processors, the standard environment of the accompanying TCP/IP subsystem contains a range of diagnostic tools and utility programs which cover most administrative tasks. This chapter explains the structure and the content of the TCP/IP configuration files on UNIX systems: the system and network administrator must know and understand these in order to install and extend the network.

# Loopback driver

The loopback driver is one of the most important help facilities for the network administrator as far as the testing of the TCP/IP subsystem is concerned.

The UNIX operating system kernel contains special software components for use by the peripherals, so-called device drivers. Within the scope of the TCP/IP subsystem, in addition to the drivers for the network connection peripherals (for example, the Ethernet controller), every UNIX system also contains a *loopback driver*. This serves a virtual (one which does not actually exist) output device whose function is to insert received data, immediately and without alteration, into an input queue to a protocol stack. In this way, local connections may be opened and the local TCP/IP system tested, without using an Ethernet controller and therefore without the influence of any hardware component.

To send data via the loopback driver, this driver must also be given an Internet network address, since it is known that packets will be sent by IP to networks. Thus, every UNIX system is a system with at least two network connections, where the virtual loopback network is however not visible from the outside. By convention, the network number of the loopback network is 127; any host ID may be chosen in it. The address of the loopback connection is entered in */etc/hosts* under the name *loopback* or *localhost* or other possible aliases.

If services cannot be accessed on one computer, the readiness of the TCP/IP system running there and of its servers may be tested using the loopback network. Thus, it is possible to determine where the problem lies. If a local connection is possible, the problem may lie in the network connection, the controller hardware or the controller driver. If the attempt is not successful, there is probably a fault in the server in question or else the problem lies in the TCP/IP subsystem of the operating system. Note that internal connections are usually set up over the Internet addresses of the real network interfaces: from a logical point of view the only difference between the two variants is that the connection is made from the viewpoint of the TCP/IP subsystem over a different Internet address.

```
# Local network host addresses
127.1              local localhost
192.9.150.202      train1
192.9.150.201      train2
0xC0.0x09.0x96.0x01 aramis   # hexadecimal
0300.011.0226.02   mitsouko # octal
```

**Figure 6.1**    Extract from */etc/hosts*.

# Configuration files in /etc

Most configuration files of the TCP/IP system on UNIX computers are found in the directory */etc*. These files contain lines of ASCII text and may be modified by any editor. The structure varies from file to file, although in all files, in each case, a line serves as a data record; comments begin with the character #.

## /etc/hosts

The purpose of the file */etc/hosts* is to provide a symbolic name for an Internet address, since, of course, users cannot be required to remember a cryptic, several-figure Internet address. An entry in */etc/hosts* consists of an Internet address in decimal, hexadecimal or octal format and an official name, as shown in Figure 6.1. In addition, one or more aliases may be given after the official name. The network administrator enters new addresses, names and aliases here when more processors are connected to the network.

When the Yellow Pages or the Domain Name Service (see next chapter) is used, the data held in this and other files is replaced or supplemented by information in the directory services. Note the interrelation of these three sources of information in possible problems associated with the addressing of computers in a network.

## /etc/networks

This file contains network names and their numbers. In some systems, many ARPA-Internet networks are listed here. The information stored is not important to most normal users and is used, as in the case of the following configuration files (see Figure 6.2), to display program output as meaningful names rather than numbers. Thus, the network administrator may enter his own network addresses and numbers here. An entry consists of network names, network numbers and alias names.

```
# network name database
loopback-net 127          software-loopback-net
ixos-net      192.9.150
```

**Figure 6.2** Extract from */etc/networks*.

## /etc/protocols

In this file, the protocol numbers of the transport protocols are entered as they appear in the transport protocol field of the IP protocol header (see Figure 6.3). This file is not altered by the administrator. The structure is as follows: protocol name, protocol number and alias name.

## /etc/services

This file contains the port numbers and the designations of existing network services (see Figure 6.4); it is read by the programs at start-up. A line consists of service name, port number and protocol type, separated by /, together with optional alias names.

## hostname

*hostname* is a simple command which tells the user the name of his own computer. This can be very useful in shell procedures. System V has a similar command called *uname*, which, among other things (with the option *−n*), returns the node name of the computer.

```
# Internet (IP) protocols
ip    0 IP   # internet protocol, pseudo protocol number
icmp  1 ICMP # internet control message protocol
ggp   3 GGP  # gateway-gateway protocol
tcp   6 TCP  # transmission control protocol
pup  12 PUP  # PARC universal packet protocol
udp  17 UDP  # user datagram protocol
```

**Figure 6.3** Extract from */etc/protocols*.

```
# Network services, Internet style
ftp     21/tcp
telnet 23/tcp
smtp    25/tcp    mail
tftp    69/udp
# UNIX-specific services
exec    512/tcp
login   513/tcp
shell   514/tcp   rcmd # no passwords used
who     513/udp   whod
```

**Figure 6.4**   Extract from */etc/services.*

The computer name is provided in the start-up files executed on system start-up. Entry of the computer name is very important since it is passed to many programs (which cannot function properly without it).

The information provided by *hostname* is insufficient for processors with access to several networks (multi-homing), since in this case an individual name should exist for each network. The name the administrator should enter is in this case open to question (he will usually choose the name most heavily used).

# netstat

The program *netstat* provides the user with comprehensive information about the state of the local TCP/IP system; thus, it is the network administrator's most important aid as far as the diagnosis of TCP/IP problems is concerned.   In 4.2/4.3BSD systems, in addition to local statements about the TCP/IP system, it also provides information about the local interprocess communication (UNIX domain), the resources of the Xerox Network System (XNS) and other active protocol stacks (manufacturer-dependent information).

*netstat* provides information about the most important TCP/IP related resources in the system:

- communication end points
- network interface statistics
- data buffers
- routing tables and statistics
- protocol statistics.

```
$ netstat −a

Active Internet connections (including servers)
Proto Recv-Q Send-Q Local Address Foreign Address (state)
tcp       0      0 aramis.login  mitsouko.1023  ESTABL.
tcp       0      0 aramis.1023   balahe.login   ESTABL.
tcp       0      0 aramis.shell  balahe.1035    TIME_WAIT
tcp       0      0 aramis.1022   balahe.1036    TIME_WAIT
tcp       0      0 *.time        *.*            LISTEN
tcp       0      0 *.daytime     *.*            LISTEN
tcp       0      0 *.portmap     *.*            LISTEN
tcp       0      0 *.chargen     *.*            LISTEN
tcp       0      0 *.discard     *.*            LISTEN
tcp       0      0 *.echo        *.*            LISTEN
tcp       0      0 *.domain      *.*            LISTEN
tcp       0      0 *.finger      *.*            LISTEN
tcp       0      0 *.exec        *.*            LISTEN
tcp       0      0 *.login       *.*            LISTEN
tcp       0      0 *.shell       *.*            LISTEN
tcp       0      0 *.telnet      *.*            LISTEN
tcp       0      0 *.ftp         *.*            LISTEN
udp       0      0 *.who         *.*
udp       0      0 *.nfs         *.*
udp       0      0 *.echo        *.*
udp       0      0 *.ntalk       *.*
udp       0      0 *.portmap     *.*
udp       0      0 *.domain      *.*
udp       0      0 *.tftp        *.*

$
```

**Figure 6.5**   Output from *netstat −a*.

## Communication end points

If no options are specified, *netstat* provides information about all active communication end points. If the option −a is given, it also provides information about passive servers.

Figure 6.5 shows two active TCP connections (ESTABLISHED) set up by *rlogin*s. The two TCP end points in the TIME_WAIT state are remnants of a completed *rsh* call and will disappear after 30 seconds (quiet time). All other end points have been opened for the server and are currently passive (LISTEN). UDP end points do not have a state. Each line shows

```
$ netstat −i
Name Mtu  Network  Address    Ipkts Ierrs Opkts Oerrs Collis
ec0  1500 ixos-net aramis     94    0     107   0     0
lo0  2048 loopback localhost  35    0     45    0     0
$ netstat −I ec0 10
     input  (ec0 )     output          input  (Total)    output
packets errs packets errs colls packets errs packets errs co
0       0    113     0    0     0       0    113     0    0
2       0    4       0    0     5       0    8       0    0
7       0    10      0    0     10      0    12      0    0
2       0    4       0    0     5       0    8       0    0
2       0    4       0    0     5       0    8       0    0
2       0    4       0    0     5       0    8       0    0
7       0    10      0    0     10      0    12      0    0
$
```

**Figure 6.6**  Output from *netstat* with options *i* and −*I*.

the local and foreign addresses of the partner. Whenever possible, the Internet address and the port number are replaced by the computer name and the name of the service. A star denotes that the end point is not yet associated with an address or that several addresses are possible. The columns Recv-Q and Send-Q show the number of bytes for this end point in the data buffer.

## Network interface statistics

A call to *netstat* with the option −*i* produces a list of the statistics of the network interface, for example, of the LAN controller driver. As Figure 6.6 shows, this list includes the number of input and output packets, the associated errors and the number of collisions on the Ethernet. Of course, for non-Ethernet controllers, the entry for the number of collisions is either empty or has another meaning (in the SLIP driver, this entry signals that memory to accept further data was exhausted). Other entries include the name of the interface (for example, 'lo0'), the maximum number of characters that a packet may contain (Mtu) (for example, 1500 for Ethernet) and the network and host addresses.

Entry of option −*I*, together with a time interval (in seconds), enables permanent monitoring of a given network interface. In this case, the sum of the statistics of all the computer interfaces and those of the monitored interface are shown for the previous time interval. This provides a clearer view of the distribution of I/O activity within the network connections.

```
$ netstat −m
alloc                inuse   total  max  fail
streams:        128    52     140   58   0
queues:         512   268     760  304   0
mblocks:       1990   134  147104  178   0
dblocks:       1592   134  145764  177   0
dblock class:
   0 (    4)    256     0   59668    4   0
   1 (   16)    256    23    3629   31   0
   2 (   64)    256     7   64586   30   0
   3 (  128)    512   103   15081  134   0
   4 (  256)    128     1    1186    5   0
   5 (  512)    128     0     570    3   0
   6 ( 1024)     32     0     638    3   0
   7 ( 2048)     16     0     403    2   0
   8 ( 4096)      8     0       3    1   0
$
```

**Figure 6.7**   Output from *netstat −m* under STREAMS.

## Data buffers

The availability of data buffers is extremely important as far as the performance of the TCP/IP system is concerned; thus, particular value is attached to evaluation of the buffer statistics in the case of problems.

For UNIX systems, there are at least two different methods of implementing TCP/IP. Firstly, there is the original implementation based on the BSD systems and, secondly, there are implementations under STREAMS. These differ mainly in their embedding into the operating system kernel, in particular in the range of various internal interfaces and functions which support this embedding. STREAMS was introduced with System V Release 3; most TCP/IP implementations under this system are portings of the BSD code to the new run-time environment. Other manufacturers have simply ported the BSD implementation, almost unchanged, to System V or are using the BSD kernel for their UNIX implementation.

Normally, these differences are not visible – for data buffer pools, BSD uses so-called mbufs, while System V STREAMS uses 'data blocks'. Since these two structures differ in their internal construction, they are also differently implemented and lead to different statistics.

Figure 6.7 shows the output of the STREAMS statistics. Statistics are given for data blocks of size from 4 to 4096 bytes and for the streamhead, queue, message-descriptor and data-descriptor tables. 'alloc' stands for the

```
$ netstat -m
156/416 mbufs in use:
        4 mbufs allocated to data
        9 mbufs allocated to packet headers
        61 mbufs allocated to socket structures
        80 mbufs allocated to protocol control blocks
        2 mbufs allocated to routing table entries
2/36 mapped pages in use
88 kbytes allocated to network (22% in use)
0 requests for memory denied
$
```

Figure **6.8**   Output from *netstat −m* under 4.2BSD.

number of blocks currently allocated, 'inuse' is the number of blocks actually used, 'total' is the total number of blocks used at any time and 'max' is the maximum number of blocks which have been simultaneously occupied at any given time. A non-zero entry in the 'fail' column means that this resource is too tightly assigned and has led to delays in, if not a refusal of, a system request (for example, for connection set-up). In this case, the number of occupied units should be increased and a new system kernel generated with modified parameters. How a system is parameterized varies from system to system – the system documentation should be read for more details.

In the 4.2/4.3BSD system, the output has a very different structure, as shown in Figure 6.8. The data buffer pool now contains only two sizes of buffer: so-called small mbufs with a usable data section of 114 bytes and mbuf clusters (mapped pages) of size 1024 bytes. A small mbuf is also required for each occupied cluster. Small mbufs are used to store socket structures (communication end points), routing table contents, protocol headers and small amounts of data. A type field specifies the purpose; Figure 6.8 shows a list of the various usage types. In this case too there are counters for occupied and free mbufs and for unsuccessful requests. Both the number of allocated buffers and the number of buffers in use are shown (for example, 156 of 416 mbufs are in use in Figure 6.8).

## Routing tables and statistics

As soon as a network is connected to other networks, the routing tables must be modified and made available for inspection. The routing table may be listed using *netstat* with the option *−r*. Option *−s* also generates the routing statistics.

```
$ netstat -r
Routing tables
Destination  Gateway    Flags  Refcnt  Use  Interface
localhost    localhost  UH     2       18   lo0
ixos-net     aramis     U      3       63   ec0
default      joop       UG     0       0    ec0
ixtrain-net  ixos       U      2       56   ec0
$ netstat -rs
routing:
       0 bad routing redirects
       0 dynamically created routes
       0 new gateways due to redirects
       0 destinations found unreachable
       0 uses of a wild card route
```

**Figure 6.9**   Output from *netstat* −r and −rs.

The list of table entries in Figure 6.9 includes the target address (the address of the network or the host to be reached through the gateway), the address of the gateway and a flag to show whether the route is active (U) and whether it leads to a host (H) or to a gateway (G). The reference counter ('Refcnt') specifies how many active connections may use a route. 'Use' contains the number of packets sent over this route. The statistics include unusable ICMP redirections and dynamically or newly (by ICMP) created, unobtainable and wild card routes. For wild card routes, packets are tentatively sent over the so-called *default* route (see *route* program).

## Protocol statistics

Finally, *netstat* may also be used with the option −s to provide the user with protocol statistics for IP, ICMP, TCP and UDP.

The TCP/IP protocol modules are implemented at many places and support counters for various situations, mostly error cases. The network administrator can use these statistics to determine if defective packets were received (whether the defective packet was produced by communication with a computer or by external effects such as an error in the communication medium). In newer implementations (4.3BSD/Tahoe), the comprehensive statistics of Figure 6.10 are extended by many entries, including, for example, the total number of TCP connections opened and closed, the number of data bytes sent, etc.

```
$ netstat -s
ip:
      102 total packets received
      0 bad header checksums
      0 with size smaller than minimum
      0 with data size < data length
      0 with header length < data size
      0 with data length < header length
      0 fragments received
      0 fragments dropped (dup or out of space)
      0 fragments dropped after timeout
      0 packets forwarded
      0 packets not forwardable
      0 redirects sent
icmp:
      6 calls to icmp_error
      0 errors not generated 'cuz old message was icmp
      Output histogram
              echo: 7
              destination unreachable: 6
      0 messages with bad code fields
      0 messages < minimum length
      0 bad checksums
      0 messages with bad length
      Input histogram
              echo reply: 7
              destination unreachable: 6
      0 message responses generated
tcp:
      0 incomplete headers
      0 bad checksums
      0 bad header offset fields
udp:
      0 incomplete headers
      0 bad data length fields
      0 bad checksums
$
```

**Figure 6.10**  Output from *netstat -s*.

```
$ /etc/ifconfig ec0
ec0:   flags=807<UP,BROADCAST,DEBUG,ARP>
    inet 192.9.150.13 netmask ffffff00 broadcast
192.9.150.255
$
```

**Figure 6.11**   Output from *ifconfig*.

# ifconfig

*ifconfig* is used to configure, activate or deactivate network interfaces such as the Ethernet controller drivers. This command may only be used by the network administrator and in the start-up files at system start-up.

In its simplest form (see Figure 6.11), *ifconfig* provides information about the current state of a network interface. In our example, the interface ec0 is active (UP), and debug mode (DEBUG) and ARP protocol (ARP) are switched on. *ec0* is also able to transmit broadcasts (BROADCAST). These entries are followed by entries for the Internet address, the broadcast address and the network mask. The network mask defines the bits of the Internet address which should be included in address comparison in routing. Normally, this is the network ID of the Internet address; for subnetwork routing the mask should be extended by the subnetwork ID.

*ifconfig* recognizes the following options and parameters:

- An address or a computer name which is entered into the interface.
- The protocol type must also be entered in 4.3BSD systems, which in addition to TCP/IP also support XNS or ISO as network protocols. If no protocol type is given, system names and addresses are interpreted by *ifconfig* as TCP/IP related.
- Interface activation.
- Interface deactivation.
- Activate or deactivate ARP usage for this interface.
- Assigns a routing-cost entry to the interface (for example, number of nodes passed through). For preference, a route with the lowest costs is chosen.
- Activation or deactivation of driver (if present) debug mode.
- Definition of the subnetwork mask for TCP/IP.
- Partner addresses for end-to-end connections.

- Definition of the broadcast address. When a program gives this target address, the interface sends a broadcast packet if possible. As a standard (from 4.3BSD), the broadcast address is the host ID with all bits set to 1; in 4.2BSD zeros were used. This option offers the facility to use existing programs, although both address variants may not be used at the same time.

- Trailer encapsulation activation or deactivation for this interface.

## arp

The network administrator uses *arp* to manage the entries in the system ARP table. Possible actions are to list, delete, enter or load from a file. Listing is per individual computer name or for the whole table, and involves the display of the Internet and Ethernet addresses and of any other known attributes of the entry.

It may, for example, be necessary to delete entries when a computer's Ethernet card is exchanged and the ARP table and the physical addresses no longer agree. In principle, every system entry determined by network enquiry is assigned a time limit, so a new Ethernet address would be automatically recognized, at the latest, on expiry of this time interval.

Values must be explicitly entered in the table if it is desired to communicate with computers which do not support ARP. Such entries may incorporate other attributes, although these are normally permanent, but like all entries however, they may be given a time limit. Thus, it is possible to make one's own processor the ARP server, thereby enabling it to reply to ARP enquiries on behalf of other (non-ARP) computers. Entries may also be read from a file, for example, when the system is booted. The Ethernet address is entered byte-wise in hexadecimal form with the individual bytes separated by colons.

## ping

Error messages such as `Connection timed out` may have a number of causes. In most cases, it is best to check first that the computer in question is active. The command *ruptime* may be used for this. Note that *ruptime* only declares a computer inactive after five minutes and that an active entry only shows that the computer in question can transmit packets. From 4.3BSD, the network administrator has another way of checking, using the command *ping*. *ping* operates at a very deep level, in that it sends out ICMP echo request calls. As long as the IP protocol module in the

```
$ ping aramis 512 10
PING aramis:  512 data bytes
520 bytes from 192.9.150.13:  icmp_seq=0.  time=20.  ms
520 bytes from 192.9.150.13:  icmp_seq=1.  time=10.  ms
520 bytes from 192.9.150.13:  icmp_seq=2.  time=10.  ms
520 bytes from 192.9.150.13:  icmp_seq=3.  time=10.  ms
520 bytes from 192.9.150.13:  icmp_seq=4.  time=10.  ms
520 bytes from 192.9.150.13:  icmp_seq=5.  time=10.  ms
520 bytes from 192.9.150.13:  icmp_seq=6.  time=10.  ms
520 bytes from 192.9.150.13:  icmp_seq=7.  time=10.  ms
520 bytes from 192.9.150.13:  icmp_seq=8.  time=10.  ms
520 bytes from 192.9.150.13:  icmp_seq=9.  time=10.  ms

——aramis PING Statistics——
10 packets transmitted, 10 packets received, 0% packet loss
round-trip (ms) min/avg/max = 10/11/20
$
```

**Figure 6.12**    Output from *ping*.

interrupted computer is still active, a reply is sent ('ICMP echo response')
showing that the computer is reachable and active. The next step is for the
network administrator to check whether the desired server is active.

*ping* sends a 64-byte packet to the given computer every second
and measures the time until the reply is received. *ping* is terminated
by entry of an abort signal from the keyboard (^C or DEL), whereupon
statistics about received and lost packets and the mean measured response
time are displayed. The time measurements are interesting in that they
indicate whether an over-long elapsed time between the two computers or
the overloading of the target computer is likely to be the underlying cause
of the problem. Normally, the response times are of the order of $\leq 10$
to 20 milliseconds. Lost packets mean that either the target computer or
the intermediate nodes have had to discard packets, whether because of
insufficient buffer space, internal jams or transmission error.

*ping* also offers a further test possibility of sending a certain number
of fixed-length packets, as shown in Figure 6.12. This enables us to
determine the behaviour for large packets. By the transmission of packets of
length greater than 1500 bytes, it provides an excellent test of the behaviour
of a computer on sending and receiving IP fragments. The option $-v$
permits the display of other received ICMP packets.

In SunOS and in some SunOS-based systems, *ping* only produces
a brief message ('XYZ is alive'). To use the facilities described here, the
option $-s$ must be used.

# trpt

In searching for obstinate errors, the TCP specialist may use the TCP trace built into the UNIX kernel. TCP trace is activated by turning on the option SO_DEBUG at the communication end point (socket) using the system call *setsockopt()*. Most of the servers described here activate TCP trace when the option −*d* is given on start-up. Subsequently, all activities relating to this communication end point are written to a ring buffer. If the variable *tcpconsdebug* in the TCP module of the UNIX operating system kernel is set to be different from the default value 0, output is generated on the system console. Generally, turning on console output is not recommended, since console output from the operating system is very inefficient and there is a danger of interrupting the operator working there.

The contents of the ring buffer may be edited and displayed using the program *trpt*. Normally, all data records in the ring buffer are analysed, but the option −*p* may be used to select and separately monitor a given connection using the address of its protocol control block. The protocol control block contains all the details of an active communication end point. The address of the protocol control block of an active connection is obtained using the *netstat* command with the option −*A*. Other options determine the details of the output and whether the program should continuously search the ring buffer for new entries. Figure 6.13 shows an application of *netstat* and *trpt* to a connection which has already been terminated. The exchange of the flag and the consequent change of state of the TCP protocol machine may be clearly traced.

In our example, SYN_SENT, ESTABLISHED, FIN_WAIT_1, FIN_WAIT_2 and TIME_WAIT denote states of the TCP protocol state machine. Before the SYN flag, which constitutes the first connection request, is sent, the state of the connection is CLOSED. It then changes to SYN_SENT, where the sender waits for the SYN to be acknowledged. The acknowledgement changes the state to ESTABLISHED while at the same time an acknowledgement is sent back to the partner of the connection. In this state, data can be transferred between the two TCPs. The sender of the first FIN flag changes its state to FIN_WAIT_1 until an acknowledgement is received, when it changes to FIN_WAIT_2, waiting for a FIN to arrive from the other end. If it arrives, it is acknowledged and the protocol state changes to TIME_WAIT. After quiet time is up, the state changes back to CLOSED.

# inetd

On the first UNIX systems with TCP/IP software, all server programs were activated at system start-up so that they could announce themselves at

```
# netstat -A
Active Internet connections
PCB       Proto Recv-Q Send-Q Local Addr.  Foreign Addr.  (state)
d1067000 tcp   0      0       aramis.1024  mitsouko.1023  TIME_WAIT

# trpt -p d1067000
d1067000:
569 SYN_SENT: output [a398dc01..a398dc05)@0(win=1000)<SYN>
    → SYN_SENT
570 SYN_SENT: input a399d601@a398dc02)<SYN,ACK> → ESTABLISHED
570 ESTABLISHED: output a398dc02@a399d602(win=fe0)<ACK>
    → ESTABLISHED
604 ESTABLISHED: input a399d602@a398dc02(win=1000)<ACK>
    → ESTABLISHED
878 FIN_WAIT_1:  output a398dc02@a399d602(win=1000)<ACK,FIN>
    → FIN_WAIT_1
879 FIN_WAIT_1:  input a399d602@a398dc03(win=fff)<ACK>
    → FIN_WAIT_2
897 FIN_WAIT_2:  input a399d602@a398dc03(win=1000)<ACK,FIN>
    → TIME_WAIT
897 TIME_WAIT: output a398dc03@a399d603(win=1000)<ACK>
    → TIME_WAIT
#
```

**Figure 6.13**  Output from *netstat* −*A* and *trpt*.

their ports and take on jobs. After a connection was made between one of these servers and a client, a child process was spawned which inherited this connection and only remained active for the duration of the connection. For its part, the central server process closed the connection immediately and waited for further new requests. This arrangement led to the start-up of between five and fifteen processes (according to the configuration) which were possibly seldom or never required.

To help matters, the program *inetd* was provided in 4.3BSD. This central 'super-server' opens the ports instead of the server program and waits for incoming connections; thus, in the inactive state only one process runs. A client-specific server process is only started when the corresponding TCP connection to the client has been established. The existing connection to the client is delivered to the server process in file descriptor 0. *inetd* is capable of starting both TCP- and UDP-based servers.

*inetd* is configured via the file */etc/inetd.cf*. Non-standard servers may also be used in this way.

```
#
# Internet server configuration database
#
ftp      stream tcp nowait root /etc/ftpd     ftpd
telnet   stream tcp nowait root /etc/telnetd  telnetd
shell    stream tcp nowait root /etc/rshd      rshd
login    stream tcp nowait root /etc/rlogind  rlogind
exec     stream tcp nowait root /etc/rexecd   rexecd
tftp     dgram  udp wait   bin  /etc/tftpd    tftpd
ntalk    dgram  udp wait   root /etc/ntalkd   ntalkd
echo     stream tcp nowait root internal
discard  stream tcp nowait root internal
chargen  stream tcp nowait root internal
daytime  stream tcp nowait root internal
time     stream tcp nowait root internal
```

**Figure 6.14**   Extract from a */etc/inetd.cf* file.

The format of an */etc/inetd.cf* entry is as follows (see Figure 6.14):

## Service name

The designation of a network service, such as *telnet*, as given in */etc/services*.

## Socket type

The type of communication mechanism (*stream*, *dgram* or *raw*).

## Protocol

*tcp* or *udp* as given in */etc/protocols*.

## wait/nowait

This is only valid for datagram servers and indicates whether *inetd* can immediately accept further connections at the same port or whether it should wait until the server has finished.

```
login tcp /etc/in.rlogind
tftp  udp /etc/in.tftpd
time  tcp /usr/etc/in.timed
rpc   udp /usr/etc/rpc.rstatd   100001 1-2
rpc   udp /usr/etc/rpc.rwalld   100008 1
rpc   udp /usr/etc/rpc.mountd   100005 1
rpc   udp /usr/etc/rpc.rusersd  100002 1-2
rpc   udp /usr/etc/rpc.sprayd   100012 1
rpc   tcp /usr/etc/rpc.rexd     100017 1
```

**Figure 6.15**  Extract from */etc/servers*.

### User name

This is the login ID under which the server should be started.

### Server program name

This is the path name of the server program. Some services are implemented internally by *inetd*.

### Parameters of the server program

These are the parameters (including the program name, parameter 0) to be delivered to the server on start-up.

Some Internet test and information services, such as *echo, discard, chargen, daytime* and *time*, are internally processed by *inetd*. These are trivial test servers which echo, consume or generate characters or return the current system time.

The configuration file is reread, possibly to make a modification effective, when the server receives a SIGHUP signal. Otherwise configuration occurs and the file is read when the system is started.

For some years, SunOS has incorporated a different form of *inetd*. In this case, at least up to SunOS 4.0, this server is controlled by the file */etc/servers*, as shown in Figure 6.15. Latterly, SunOS also has a 4.3BSD compatible *inetd* and a file */etc/inetd.cf*. In addition, the SunOS server is also able to start up RPC servers. This also involves registering the RPC service with the port mapper; thus, */etc/servers* and the file */etc/inetd.cf* (syntactically extended in SunOS) also contain entries for the RPC program and version numbers.

# Internetworking

## 7

- Gateways, bridges and routers
- Routing
- Domain Name Service
- Network management

Among the most important functions of a network architecture are the ability to switch packets between different sections of the network and the possibility of addressing network objects using symbolic names. Over recent years, the subject of network management has also increased in importance with the widespread introduction of networks and the increase in network sizes. The TCP/IP architecture was conceived for large and very large networks; it is currently the only manufacturer-independent architecture which can be said to have been proven in this context for some years. If you are planning to install a network which is larger than a single Ethernet segment, you should devote your attention in this chapter to the relevant concepts and the possibilities offered by the Internet architecture and the implementation on your UNIX computer.

## Gateways, bridges and routers

In discussions about networks, the term 'gateway' is often used in one context or another. Since however so-called gateway functions are implemented in very different ways, we shall look at the individual criteria for distinguishing them. Firstly, the dictionary definition (Schneider, 1983): [A gateway is] a communication processor between different computer networks whose job it is to transmit messages from one network to another network. One important aspect is protocol conversion. A gateway is usually realized using a special-purpose computer. Protocol conversion (protocol translation) usually takes place at the line and transport protocol levels.

Admittedly, transitions between the modes of operation of a switching computer are in practice often smooth; thus, we shall restrict ourselves to basics.

### Routers

A router is usually defined to be a node in the network which forwards packets in a lower layer without a protocol change occurring in that layer. Routers operate at the network level, which in our case means the IP level. There may well be a protocol change in the underlying layers, for example, a transition from Ethernet to SLIP and RS232. Either a UNIX computer with several network connections or a stand-alone specialized processor, as offered by some manufacturers, may be used as a router. Internet routers are capable of taking routing decisions based on information in the IP protocol header and in their routing tables. As Figure 7.1 shows, only OSI layers 1 to 3 need be implemented in a router.

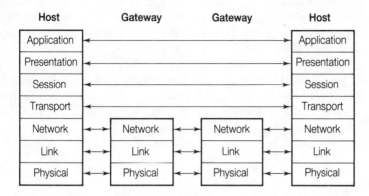

**Figure 7.1**  Communication between the layers of the OSI model.

## Bridges

Bridges are nodes which link together (almost 'extend') two segments of a network over large distances. Usually, two bridges are linked by a serial line, for example, a leased line or X.25. A separate protocol is used on this line to transport packets from one segment to the other.

Bridges may operate in the network as Internet routers (B- routers). For LANs, usually only so-called *MAC layer bridges* (from Media Access Control) are used to receive data from the link layer of a LAN segment (for example, Ethernet) and to forward it to another LAN segment. MAC layer bridges do not carry out routing, since this activity takes place below the network layer in OSI level 3. An 'intelligent' or 'learning' MAC bridge does however 'listen in' to dynamically construct internal tables containing entries for stations connected to the segment. Thus, the bridge itself knows which packets must be transmitted between the segments. If a station sends a packet to an address in the other segment, the bridge automatically forwards the packet without being prompted or noticed by the sender station. MAC bridges are very popular since they are efficient and easy to install and to configure. In addition, they have the advantage of being independent of the protocol architectures used in a LAN.

## Gateways

Gateways or relays are stations which link together two different protocols or protocol hierarchies and thus execute a conversion of the protocol. Examples of commercial gateways are the special-purpose computers through which Macintoshs on the Apple LocalTalk LAN communicate with

UNIX processors and NFS as file server. Here, relay functions are directly executed at several points: on adapting to the subnetwork medium (Apple LocalTalk → Ethernet) and on conversion of the network and transport layer protocols and of the file access protocol (Apple Filing Protocol → NFS).

In the TCP/IP literature, the term gateway is generally used for a router in the sense of the above definition. We shall adopt this definition for the purposes of discussion in the following sections.

# Routing

## Basic principles

*Routing* means that a packet must initially be sent through one or more nodes in order to reach another computer. This means that we must enter on one computer the address of the computer which provides for the transfer into the remote network, or which at least forwards the packet towards another computer. The latter may possibly pass the packet to the destination or itself forward it further. Networks with this capability are called *packet-switched networks*. There are also message- and line-switched networks. In the former, completely self-contained message units (for example, files in the *UNIX-to-UNIX copy* (UUCP) network) are transmitted; in the second case, fixed connections (as for example in a telephone circuit) are switched. Packet-switched networks have the advantage over line-switched networks that they share the physically existing network among all the connected computers and thus use the network more efficiently. The round trip time for packet-switched networks is shorter than that for message-switched networks and thus makes on-line operation possible. However, packet-switched networks are a great deal more complicated to plan, install and operate, since various problems (for example, line failure or shifts in load behaviour) must be compensated for.

Most of the complexity of a packet-switched network lies in the mechanism by which its routing tables are constructed. There are various ways of constructing routing tables in gateways:

(1) Fixed routing tables which are generated during configuration of the network and which may only be altered by restarting the node. This method is very inflexible in respect of changes in the network configuration.

(2) Loading of the table during operation through a central routing control point. This is much more flexible than method 1, but also very susceptible: if failures occur in the network, it may in

certain circumstances be impossible to load a table needed to remedy matters, since the node is unreachable.

(3) Dynamic adaptation of the table by evaluating messages on the fly and/or by interchange of information with the neighbour gateway. This method is the one which is most frequently used in Internet. It permits a self-contained and rapid adaptation of the routing table to changes in external circumstances.

A prerequisite for performance of the gateway function is that a computer must be physically connectable to at least two networks. As a rule, this is the case in TCP/IP implementations which are embedded in UNIX operating systems. Intelligent controllers which run TCP/IP, so-called 'front ends', may usually only be connected to a single network.

## Gateway protocols

Gateways must exchange information about the other networks to which they have access. *Gateway protocols* are used for this purpose.

It has not been shown to be advantageous for all networks in the Internet (there could be several thousand at some time) to use the same routing algorithm. It is far better to allow networks under certain circumstances to use algorithms adapted to their own requirements. Moreover, malfunctioning of a gateway should not endanger the remainder of the network, even if this gateway sends faulty routing information.

Since networks should be available for through traffic, as before, a procedure for free information exchange (under certain conditions) must be implemented. This relates solely to the communication between networks; other prerequisites apply to internal network information exchange.

For semantic reasons, we now introduce a new term: that of the *autonomous system*. An autonomous system may be defined to be any subnetwork of the Internet whose structure is transparent from the outside. As far as relationships between gateways are concerned, according to the definition of an autonomous system, distinction is made between so-called *interior neighbours* (gateways which are resident within the same autonomous system) and *exterior neighbours* (gateways of different autonomous systems). This relationship is shown diagrammatically in Figure 7.2. Networks 1 and 2 are both autonomous systems with two exterior neighbours and the computers A and B as interior neighbours.

Message exchange between the exterior gateways is through the *Exterior Gateway Protocol* (EGP) as specified in RFC 827 (Rosen, 1982), RFC 888 (Sämonson and Rosen, 1984) and RFC 904 (Mills, 1984). The

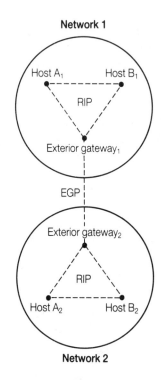

**Figure 7.2**    The Internet routing concept.

concept of the autonomous system and of the neighbour computer is also described in these documents.

Non-gateway computers must be aware of the routes available to them. The most popular protocol for message exchange within an autonomous system is the *Routing Information Protocol* (RIP) developed by the University of California in Berkeley and specified in RFC 1058 (Hedrick, 1988). It was first implemented in the program *routed* in 4.2BSD. There is also the HELLO protocol, specified in RFC 891 (Mills, 1983), which incorporates other functions (for example, synchronization of the clocks of the computers in the network) in addition to the exchange of routing information. While EGP is as a rule only used in the Internet, where autonomous systems (connections between large networks) exist, RIP is also important in private networks with internal gateways, in which it is much used. HELLO is only available on a few processors and is thus not very common.

All three protocols are based on the regular exchange of information (usually every 30 seconds); EGP establishes logical connections with neighbour gateways, while RIP broadcasts its messages into the network.


## Route, routed and gated

In every TCP/IP system (even those which cannot be connected to more than one physical network), it is possible to specify routes into other networks. This is done by an entry in an internal system routing table, either manually, using the command *route*, or automatically by the dæmon *routed* (which is available on almost all systems) or via *gated* (which is only found on a few systems).

Both *routed* and *gated* are able to exchange RIP protocol messages with other dæmons. In this way, they inform interior neighbours about the routes available on their own system and find out about existing routes in other networks, which routes they then enter in their own routing table. However, both dæmons are only used in networks containing gateways. There, for the purposes of automatic route entry, they should be active on all computers. In addition to RIP, *gated* can also process the EGP and HELLO protocols, taking into account the mutual effects the three protocols may have on one another. A separate implementation of EGP is available in the *public domain* and is described in RFC 991 (Kirton, 1984).

*route* can only manipulate one route per call. *routed* and *gated* may be used to specify static routes which are automatically entered into the routing table on system start-up. *gated* also allows the network administrator to decide which gateways are to be trusted, since the reliability of the entries in the exchanged protocol messages influences the robustness of the whole route configuration. *routed* reads static route entries from the file */etc/gateways*, while *gated* is configured from the file */etc/gated.cf*.

For message exchange over a route to be operational, the route must be entered in both directions. If this is not done then, while the target processor will be able to receive messages, it will not be able to send its reply back, so that, for example, set-up is not possible over TCP. A new route should be tested using the command *ping* in both directions.

It is very practical to enter a *default* route in the routing table. This route has Internet address 0.0.0.0 and indicates a gateway. All packets with unknown Internet target addresses are first sent to this gateway, in the hope that the latter knows the remainder of the route and in certain circumstances returns an ICMP redirect with the Internet address of the required gateway. If the gateway is unable to forward the packet, it returns an ICMP message of type 'Destination Unreachable'.

# Domain Name Service

## Background

When we execute TCP/IP programs, we usually address the desired computer with a symbolic name. The network-wide mapping of symbolic computer names to Internet addresses was made centrally for the Internet in the file HOSTS.TXT on the NIC computer. This file had to be regularly read using FTP by all computers connected to the Internet. The local copies of this file for the connected computers were found in */etc/hosts*.

Over recent years, Internet has grown from a few hundred to several thousand computers. In view of this, it is increasingly difficult to keep the information in HOSTS.TXT constantly up to date, since there are ongoing alterations. In addition, because of its size, file transfer required considerable time and overloaded the network. The solution to this problem could only be a service which shifted the management of the data away from the centre to the originator of alterations and thus to organizations which operate parts of the network. This idea gave rise to the Domain Name Service (DNS), the Internet *directory service*. The term 'directory service' is usually applied to the case in which applications and users can retrieve information stored under a name. In our case, the information may include Internet addresses, port numbers and mailboxes, as in a telephone directory. Another directory service supported on UNIX computers is the Yellow Pages service, now termed *Network Information Service* (NIS), which is incorporated in NFS.

The concepts and protocols of the Internet DNS are described in RFC 1034 (Mockapetris, 1987a) and RFC 1035 (Mockapetris, 1987b). In 4.3BSD, an implementation of this specification on UNIX systems was made available. The program *named* is a DNS-compatible *name server*. Its query section, called the *resolver*, is implemented in the form of library routines which are linked into a program.

The procedure for participating in the world-wide DNS with one's own network is described in RFC 1032 (Stahl, 1987).

## Structure of the name space

As the name DNS indicates, the name space of the network is divided into domains. The domains are arranged in a tree structure; there is a root and above that are so-called *top-level domains*, which are again subdivided into subdomains.

Figure 7.3 shows part of the DNS. A domain is referred to by specifying a path from the branch in the direction of the root, for example,

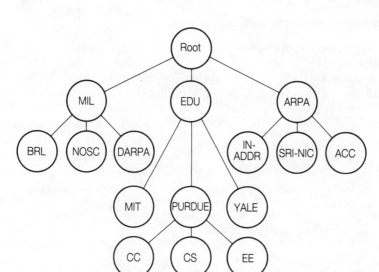

**Figure 7.3**   Extract from the domain name space.

CS.PURDUE.EDU. At the ends of the branches are addressable objects such as host computers and mailboxes. The names of these objects are always unique with a domain.

The top-level domains are predefined by the NIC; they are user domains in the USA. Currently, these include:

- MIL for the US military.
- EDU for universities and other educational organizations.
- GOV for government organizations.
- COM for commercial industrial organizations.
- ORG for non-commercial organizations.
- ARPA for Internet-specific organizations.

In addition to these top-level domains for organizations within the USA, there is a top-level domain for each connected country, for example, DE for Germany and UK for Great Britain. In some countries, the national top-level domain includes a subdomain structure similar to that of the top-level domain in the USA.

## DNS name servers

DNS name servers manage so-called zones. A zone begins at a node in the DNS tree and contains all underlying branches. A name server may now delegate authority over a subzone to another name server and thus control the sources of information in a subdomain. DNS consists of a large number of nested zones, in which name servers operate. These name servers each recognize their neighbour servers in the zones immediately above and below. For reasons of reliability, each zone has at least two active name servers (*primary* and *secondary*), which both provide the same information.

Information about addressable objects is stored in *Resource Records* (RRs), which are managed by name servers. User programs generate RR queries via the resolver. RRs consist of the following fields:

- owner of the information
- type
- class (for example, IN for Internet, ISO for ISO)
- period of validity
- data.

The syntax used for RRs in the name server databases is fully specified (Mockapetris, 1987b). The data is coded in ASCII and may therefore be exchanged between name servers without conversion. The name server databases include the following available RR types:

- *Start of Authority (SOA)*: Definition of a zone.
- *Address (A)*: Internet address of a host.
- *Name Server (NS)*: Name of a name server for a domain.
- *Host Information (HINFO)*: Entries relating to the operating system, hardware, etc.
- *Canonical Name (CNAME)*: Alias for a computer.
- *Well-Known Services (WKS)*: List of services provided (TELNET, FTP, SMTP, etc.).
- *Mail Exchanger (MX)*: A mail manager for a domain.
- *Gateway Pointer (PTR)*: Gateway addresses.

Queries and replies to queries consist of four variable-length fields:

- A query field used to specify the information required.
- An answer field containing the required information.
- If the name server is unable to supply the information, the AUTHORITY field contains the names of authorized name servers

which do have the information.

- An additional field for further (optional) information for the initiator of the query, for example, the address of the name server given in the AUTHORITY field.

## Resolver

The resolver takes over name server queries on behalf of the application program and thus also on behalf of the user. The resolver is required (as far as possible) to store the information obtained locally (caching), so that this information may be used in similar queries without the need for further communication with the name server. The storage period depends on the period of validity specified in the RR, which determines the length of time the resolver should temporarily hold the information in the absence of a renewed request for it.

A resolver should also be able to settle so-called *iterative queries* and thus to forward queries which cannot be successfully answered by a name server, using the information in its AUTHORITY field, by contacting other name servers. It can however also request the name server to execute this so-called iterative query, in which case the name server is responsible for the subsequent forwarding (this implies an increased load on the name server).

The UNIX resolver available in 4.3BSD is a very limited implementation which cannot execute either local caching or iterative queries. However, both these functions are implemented in the BIND server (see later) and, moreover, the resolver is configured in such a way that queries outside of the domain pass to the name server. The resolver is designed to be a transparent replacement for existing routines to search the files in */etc* (such as */etc/hosts*); thus, as a rule, a program must only be linked to a new subroutine library and need not be altered.

For queries, the resolver may use either UDP or TCP, where UDP, as the standard protocol, has its own error protection (repetition of query). Iterative queries may under certain circumstances take a long time, so care should be taken to ensure that the repetitions are not sent too soon. If this is not possible, TCP should be used. These facilities in the UNIX resolver are configurable by the user individually.

If the NFS NIS and DNS are used at the same time, there may be overlaps in the information supplied by the two services (for example, in the system addresses). Some systems contain entries in the resolver's configuration file which point the resolver to maps of NIS.

## BIND

The *Berkeley Internet Name Domain* (BIND) server incorporated in 4.3BSD is a complete implementation of the DNS for UNIX systems. It is available under the program name *named* and is configured from a number of files.

It executes caching and iterative queries and may be configured in three different modes: as a primary server, a secondary server or a caching-only server. In the last case, the server does not manage a database of its own, but, as mentioned earlier, only takes over functions which the resolver itself is unable to execute. Even caching-only servers must not be started on every processor: the resolver may be configured in such a way that it is possible to contact up to three different non-local name servers.

# Network management

As the size of networks increases, network management (the administration of hosts and gateways in the network) is an increasing challenge. The task of network management is to monitor the elements of the network in order to identify malfunctions (for example, due to capacity bottlenecks), faults or structural changes at an early stage and to take countermeasures. In some network architectures, this also includes the control of access to the network and the allocation of information for metered accounting.

Although there is a whole range of programs for local management of the TCP/IP subsystem, and although network management protocols to manage the Internet Message Processor (IMP) in the original BBN ARPANET have already been introduced in practice, promising activities as far as general network-wide management protocols in the Internet are concerned have only been undertaken in the last three years. Some implementations have been demonstrated in practice, but are very rarely found on UNIX systems.

Network management is an area in which evolution is still rife. Based on early attempts to define the functions and the management information base for network management, the IAB has decided on a strategy which permits a gradual transition to the network management protocols defined by ISO (Cerf, 1988). These activities come under the keywords *Common Management Over TCP* (CMOT), specified in RFC 1095 (Warrier and Besaw, 1989), where common management refers to ISO specifications for *Common Management Information Service Definition* (CMIS) (ISO/IEC 9595) and *Common Management Information Protocol* (CMIP) (ISO/IEC 9596).

During the transition period, initial experience should be gained using the *Simple Network Management Protocol* (SNMP) specified in RFC 1157 (Davin *et al.*, 1990). SNMP is used to exchange data between the SNMP agent (the computer being managed) and the network management station (the manager). The information available to the network manager in the SNMP agent is defined in the *Management Information Base* (MIB) in RFCs 1155 and 1156 (McCloghrie and Rose, 1990a and b). SNMP may be used for queries relating to entries in the routing table, the state of network interfaces, protocol statistics and much else. In addition, the network administrator may also make alterations to specifically authorized MIB entries from the outside. Thus, he may authorize the SNMP agent to inform him when a computer is newly started, a network interface is activated or deactivated, or a connection to an exterior neighbour gateway is lost. The information exchange in the MIB will usually be encoded according to the *Abstract Syntax Notation One* (ASN.1) (ISO, 1987a and b).

It is assumed that SNMP will establish itself as a viable standard for the years to come. Since large manufacturers in particular have for some considerable time solved the network management problem for their clients with their own mature network architectures, it is clear that when these clients transfer to open systems (including TCP/IP) they will demand a similar functionality. If the critical mass is achieved, the rest of the market will be drawn along and will also offer SNMP functionality. As more managed objects (that is, elements in an MIB) are defined by the various standards bodies, the CMOT architecture will increase in importance, since it provides better support than SNMP for more complex MIBs.

# 8

# Introduction to NFS

- Presentation of the NFS technology
- Steps to network integration
- Alternatives to NFS

This chapter begins the second part of the book on the *Network File System* (NFS). First, we shall consider the NFS technology generally, there then follows a brief discussion of the scope and applications. Finally, we look at two of the most important networked file systems.

# Presentation of the NFS technology

NFS was developed and brought to the market by Sun Microsystems Inc. Sun is primarily a manufacturer of UNIX workstations, but it has also been one of the strongest forces in the UNIX movement over recent years.

Sun Microsystems has taken on board the philosophy of distributed and open systems. Thus, from the beginning, NFS was designed so that it permitted the connection of computers from different manufacturers with very different operating systems running on them. Naturally, this philosophy was not followed without some selfishness. Sun only produces workstations, which are primarily used in networks with systems from other manufacturers. Nevertheless, the fact that NFS could be used in heterogeneous network environments was probably its greatest advantage over other products, such as AT&T's *Remote File System* (RFS: see 'Alternatives to NFS' at the end of this chapter).

Set against previous customs, in which manufacturers produced new developments for their own hardware platforms alone, in the hope of binding clients to a computer system, Sun has trodden a completely new road. The specifications of the NFS protocol have been published and a reference implementation for UNIX is available to all interested parties at a favourable price (in comparison with its cost). Most manufacturers of UNIX systems have ported this reference system, or a variant of it, to their computers and pay licence fees to Sun. Thus, at least in the UNIX world, NFS has become the *de facto* standard for distributed file access and is today available for practically every UNIX system. It is even conjectured that in the future a UNIX system without NFS will have no chance in the market. NFS is a component of the System V Release 4 of December 1989 and is thus incorporated in the *System V Interface Definition* (SVID).

A few manufacturers and software houses have used the published specifications to implement the NFS protocol themselves and to integrate it into their products. These products may be operated without a licence and may be made public. The new 4.4BSD UNIX version also contains a reimplementation of NFS, as does OSF/1, the Open Software Foundation's implementation of UNIX.

## Modes of application and operation

NFS is usually supplied as an extension of the operating system offered by the manufacturer and must be acquired as an add-on. Most technical workstations are exceptions to this and include NFS and TCP/IP protocols and commands as part of the basic configuration. This trend will increase with the integration of NFS into System V and other leading UNIX derivatives and with the imminent networking of all workstations and personal computers. NFS products are available for operating systems other than UNIX, for example, for MS-DOS, VMS, MVS, etc.

NFS allows programs read and write access to files on NFS server computers. This access is transparent to the programs, which need no alteration, special preparation or additional parameters before operating over NFS. The files on the NFS server are made accessible in that the NFS client computer mounts individual file systems (or sections) from file systems of the NFS server into its own file system. The allocation of these access capabilities is not usually made in response to a request from the program desiring the access but must be granted to the local system before the access is made.

One aspect of this transparency is the speed of the data access over the network, which must be so high that there is no noticeable difference from a local disk access. The original goal in developing NFS was to achieve 80% of the data throughput rate for a fixed local disk. Thus, it is possible that access over NFS to a dedicated NFS server with a very fast fixed disk may, under certain circumstances, attain a better throughput than that possible locally on a computer with a cheap but slow fixed disk. High-grade optimized workstations, in particular those which may be operated without a local fixed disk, may commonly have read or write speeds in excess of several hundred kilobytes per second over NFS.

NFS implementations on UNIX systems with local fixed disks can usually operate symmetrically; thus, a processor may be a client and a server at the same time. Two computers may thus share their files, provided this is permitted by the network administrator for the given configuration. Depending on the NFS implementation and on the nature of the operating system, most non-UNIX systems only allow a specific mode of operation. Integration of the NFS client into an operating system is much more complicated than the implementation of a server. Thus, manufacturers of mainframe and mini computers mostly offer server implementations which make good use of the fixed-disk storage space which is generally plentiful on these systems. For PCs, client implementations are almost always the rule, since the allocation and management of disk space for a large number of PCs is most cheaply achieved using a central server. Since MS-DOS (which is predominant on PCs) only permits *single-tasking*, it is impossible to use client and server programs simultaneously.

NFS is sometimes termed a *distributed file system*. A more correct terminology would be 'network file system' which in any case is the meaning of the initials NFS. NFS does not distribute file systems in the network, but converts local accesses into requests to one or more servers.

This concept is not new; it has already been successfully used in many other systems. Many such solutions have been developed for UNIX systems over the last ten years. Network file systems have also been implemented for other operating systems, in particular for PCs and the MS-DOS operating system.

## Genesis

NFS was announced in 1984. The first implementation on a Sun workstation was introduced in the next year. This product had version number 2.0 and contained a client and server implementation within the new *Virtual File System* (VFS), a framework for incorporating file systems into UNIX, and the directory service then called *Yellow Pages* (YP).

In 1986, the firms The Instruction Set Ltd and Lachman Associates Inc ported the reference implementation of NFS Version 2.0 to System V Release 2 for a DEC VAX. This porting was needed since the Sun reference implementation was based on 4.2BSD from which SunOS also descended. The porting to System V showed that it was possible to make NFS available on practically all UNIX computers. In the same year, Sun issued a new version of NFS, Version 3.0, which was distinguished from its predecessors mainly through improvements to the YP protocol. In addition, Sun also released the first implementation of NFS for PCs under MS-DOS (PC-NFS) in the same year.

Version 3.2 was introduced in 1987. As a major extension, this offered the possibility of network-wide file locking, a function which had been requested by many users since the start. It also incorporated the *Remote Execution Service* (REX), a network service enabling one to initiate processes on other machines; these processes then accessed local files via NFS. In addition, NFS support for diskless workstations was improved to allow them to be supported using special files and named pipes. In the same year, Lachman Associates Inc ported NFS to System V Release 3 under the *File System Switch* (FSS).

Version 4.0 of NFS, released in 1989, contains encryption facilities which may be used to guarantee that file access cannot be spoofed. In 1989, NFS was licensed to more than 260 manufacturers.

## Product and protocol

In considering NFS, we must distinguish between the NFS product and the NFS protocol:

- The NFS product consists of a range of protocols incorporating very different functions. Other tasks must be accomplished in the network, in addition to file access (for example, in the management area). NFS usually defines a separate protocol for each of these tasks.

The components of an NFS product and its application are discussed in Chapter 10.

- The NFS protocol is a protocol within the NFS product which is used to access files and which has given its name to the NFS product. We shall discuss NFS and other protocols in more detail in the next chapter.

The following criteria may be used to prove that two individual implementations are compatible:

- The protocols used in the NFS product have version numbers; only implementations with the same version of the protocol are compatible.
- The functional scope of the NFS product on a UNIX computer is not specified. Individual manufacturers decide which protocols, programs and commands are implemented. As a rule, manufacturers are guided by the most recent version of NFS for Sun workstations.

As we shall show, there are trivial, mostly system-specific, differences between versions from different manufacturers.

# Steps to network integration

## Principles

Since the breakthrough of the so-called *time-sharing* principle in commercial operating systems, networking in electronic data processing has greatly increased. Central processing is increasingly being replaced by desktop PCs or workstations. In what follows, we shall discuss the possible steps towards integration in a network.

### Step 1: Time Sharing

The most widespread method of data access which is heavily predominant in the area of large-scale, serial computers involves a central processor in which all the data is stored and which handles all applications. In this case, the resources are not distributed over a network. UNIX systems are constructed according to this principle. The disadvantages of this are the capacity limits of the central processor, since when this is fully loaded an extension may be expensive or technically impossible. The suitability of the central computer may be another problem. There may be important reasons against migrating new applications to a computer which is already in operation, for example, security requirements, availability of special applications, graphical capabilities, etc.

### Step 2: File transfer

This step refers to the transfer of all the data to another computer, for example, using FTP. The processing takes place locally, on the same computer on which the processing application runs. It is basically unimportant whether the file transfer is carried out over a network or using a storage medium such as a floppy disk. Both cases involve the problem that the file may be altered on each computer and thus at times the copies will differ from the most recent state. These differences must be eliminated by a periodic and possibly complicated procedure.

### Step 3: File access in the network

In this case, NFS (for example) is used to access individual blocks of a central file, where the data structures are interpreted in the processing computer. The same is true for the writing of data – files are in principle modified centrally. There is another difference from file transfer, namely, that only the section of a file which is required at that moment is transmitted. However, as a prerequisite, all applications which access the file must expect an identical file structure.

### Step 4: Data queries in the network

This involves structured access to individual data records using a query language such as the *Structured Query Language* (SQL). In this case, the data is pre-selected in the server according to criteria specified in the query; thus, only the relevant data within a file is transmitted. The level of abstraction is higher than that in step 3; instead of files, the server manages and stores logical entities, possibly in an optimal manner.

Each of these steps towards integration has implications on the cost. This must be in keeping with the requirements.

## Fields of application of NFS

Like all mechanisms, file access in the network has its advantages and disadvantages which consequently determine the preferred applications and scope.

NFS permits optional access to file blocks in the form in which they are stored on the fixed disk, without interpretation of the internal structure; thus, it operates 100% according to the UNIX philosophy which leaves these tasks to the application programs. Since index sequential files are implemented differently in each operating system, the developers of NFS have not attempted to incorporate a high-level access mechanism for this either.   For these reasons, the operation of UNIX databases over NFS, while possible, is unreasonable, since all the index information must be transmitted over the network in order to find the required data. An additional factor is the throughput rate for the necessary locking of individual data records in the case of multiple access, which is decreased when a network is used.   It is better in this case to install a database with distributed access on a central database server; this amounts to step 4 integration as currently offered by database manufacturers.

The preferred application areas for NFS are development, design and office automation, where common data in the form of source-code files, object libraries, letters, etc. is accessed.   In combination with a database server, the most appropriate access mechanism is used for each type of data.

# Alternatives to NFS

Naturally, as a product, NFS has competitors. In particular, integration of MS-DOS systems will certainly not be achieved by equipping all PCs with PC-NFS. In this section, we look at two products which are similarly used in local area networks on UNIX systems, in addition to a product which is currently being developed.

## RFS

The Remote File System (RFS) was released by AT&T together with the System V Release 3 in 1986.   This system has never been as successful as NFS, one reason being that NFS reached the market two years earlier.   Another reason may have been the inept licensing politics for System V Release 3 with which AT&T pushed the thoroughly desirable standardization of UNIX rather too blatantly for the taste of their competitors. Without going further into the protocols used by RFS and its implementation, we shall briefly look at the differences between RFS and NFS using a keyword list:

- *Functionality from the user's viewpoint*: Almost identical to NFS. Both products offer transparent networking and are not visible to the user and his applications. In RFS also, file systems are locally mounted on the server computer. Unlike NFS, RFS also permits access to special files.

- *Support for diskless systems*:   Not catered for.   Although in principle possible, RFS incorporates no arrangements to provide an implementation for diskless systems.

- *Management*: Conceptually, semantically and syntactically different. Roughly speaking, the RFS subsystem is managed by a computer designated for this purpose, while an NFS network, with the exception of NIS, consists of independently managed computers.

- *Use in non-UNIX environments*: Unlike NFS, RFS is solely designed for use on UNIX systems. Integration with MS-DOS, VMS or other operating systems is practically impossible. However, the UNIX systems used in RFS networks may be based on various processor architectures.

- *Preservation of the UNIX file system – semantics*: Better than NFS. The RFS protocol does not use file access primitives but issues UNIX system calls to dynamically generated processes in the server computer. This also enables access to special files.

- *Performance*: Determined by configuration. Connection-oriented transport protocols are generally used, which leads to higher processing costs. The packet size used is generally smaller than in NFS.

- *Independence from the transport protocols used*: High. The RFS modules use the *Transport Level Interface* (TLI) and the *Transport Provider Interface* (TPI) in System V. Below these interfaces any protocol hierarchies within the STREAMS architecture may be used.

- *Security*: Better than NFS. As in NFS, user and group IDs are used as authentication information. However, these IDs may be protected against overlapping or deactivated using conversion tables in the server.

- *Protection against failure*: Worse than NFS. A transparent restart after a server crash is not possible.

- *Openness*: The RFS source code is available under a System V licence. However, AT&T has never published the protocols.

System V Release 4 will permit the coexistence of RFS and NFS.

## LAN Manager/X

Anyone interested in the networking of PCs will surely be familiar with the terms PC-NET, MS-NET, NETBIOS and LAN Manager. These terms stand for a technology created by the two protagonists of the MS-DOS world, IBM and MicroSoft.

PC-NET and MS-NET enable a PC to access a dedicated server computer, in that they make the server's file system appear to the client as a virtual additional disk drive. Both contain a *redirector*, a software module which converts accesses to this disk drive into messages to the server, which has been integrated into MS-DOS since 1985. The protocol used for this is called the *Server Message Block* (SMB); its messages are sent via calls to another interface, the NETBIOS. NETBIOS defines an interface which must serve implementations of transport protocols in order to work with PC-NET. Many manufacturers also supply NETBIOS-compatible network software, including software for TCP/IP.

Over recent years, the SMB protocol has evolved considerably, and we now speak of Core-SMB and the Extended-SMB-protocol, where the latter is upwards compatible. The Extended-SMB-protocol contains extensions for the networking of UNIX and/or OS/2 computers. A UNIX-to-UNIX file system based on the SMB protocol was once offered in the mid eighties in the form of the XENIX-NET product. Because of the dominance of NFS and RFS, this product had little success and disappeared from the market. However, it was the first product capable of serving MS-DOS client PCs with a UNIX server. For OS/2, the LAN manager (and with it SMB) is the strategic network product.

LAN Manager/X is a new implementation of the Extended-SMB-protocol for UNIX systems produced by the companies MicroSoft and Hewlett-Packard. It is a server-only implementation; thus, the LAN Manager/X cannot be used to network together UNIX systems. But, since it is implemented as a normal user program, it can make use of the networking facilities available on UNIX systems, in that it can access another UNIX processor over NFS-mounted file systems. In addition to file access, the LAN Manager/X also supports access to communication lines and interprocess communication between programs on the PC and UNIX together with the print output on the server.

The fact that access to the LAN Manager/X appears transparent to applications running on the PC is self-evident. When it comes to the authentication of clients, the LAN Manager, like its predecessors, follows a different route to NFS. Since MS-DOS itself knows no user names (whose IDs it could send to the server), when the disk drive is mounted, a type of session is initiated in the server during which the user authenticates his own identity, possibly with a password (this is practically a login). All activities subsequently initiated by the PC user then occur under the authority of his user name on the UNIX server. Thus, there is a correlation between PC and UNIX user names.

MS-DOS also has a hierarchical file system at its disposal, but unlike UNIX it uses a backslash (or '\') to separate individual components of a path name for subsequent conversion by the LAN Manager/X. It is difficult to integrate access to UNIX files whose names exceed the usual length in MS-DOS (up to eight characters with three characters after the full stop as an extension). Moreover, this system does not distinguish between lower- and upper-case letters in file names; even though the LAN Manager/X in principle converts such entries into lower-case, file names such as *Makefile* and *makefile* naturally cause problems. The solution chosen in the LAN Manager/X is very simple: files which cannot be unambiguously referenced remain invisible to the PC user.

To summarize, it is clear that the LAN Manager/X fully covers the rich functionality of the Extended-SMB-protocol. Using this, UNIX systems may be completely transparently integrated into existing PC networks.

## DFS

As of writing, the OSF is preparing a distributed file system service called DFS which is based on the *Andrew File System* developed at the Carnegie Mellon University, but which contains many improvements on the original design.

Since DFS is not yet commercially available, we can only speculate that it will be a strong contender in the area of distributed file systems, since it solves many of NFS's most obvious problems, such as data integrity, security, etc. Based on a client/server architecture, it uses tokens between clients and servers to mediate concurrent access to files and to provide improved client caching. Integration with other DCE services like X.500 and Kerberos authentication should provide the basis for the operation of an efficient, reliable and secure world-wide file system.

# 9

# NFS protocols

- Classification of NFS protocols
- Remote Procedure Call
- External Data Representation
- Port mapper
- Network File System protocol
- MOUNT protocol
- Network Information Service

**Figure 9.1**   Comparison of OSI and NFS protocol layers.

In this chapter, we look at the most important protocols of the NFS technology and consider their characteristics. The corresponding commands and their functional descriptions will be discussed in the next chapter.

This split has been made in order to confine the description of the overall operation of NFS as far as is possible to a single chapter and to separate this clearly from more theoretical considerations of the protocols. Thus, there will be many references to the attributes described in this chapter.

## Classification of NFS protocols

NFS is based on a protocol layering which largely corresponds to the layering defined in the OSI model (see Figure 9.1). Being modelled on OSI, NFS is theoretically protocol independent. Every layer of the protocol hierarchy may be exchanged for a functionally identical variant with no negative consequences for the rest of the system. In practice, however, all implementations currently on the market incorporate the same protocols.

Table 9.1 lists the relevant standards for the protocols used in NFS. Additional variants are only offered in some cases where LAN technology is used; thus, for example, IBM NFS may be operated over token ring (in fact, the functional differences between token ring and Ethernet are small). NFS is based on the protocols TCP/IP since these are very common

Table **9.1**   NFS protocol standards.

| Layer | Protocols | Standard |
|-------|-----------|----------|
| Physical/Link | CSMA/CD | Ethernet IEEE 802.3 |
| Network | IP | RFC 791 |
| Transport | TCP | RFC 793 |
| | UDP | RFC 768 |
| Session | RPC | RFC 1050 |
| Presentation | XDR | RFC 1014 |
| Application | NFS MOUNT | RFC 1094 |
| | YP YPBIND REX NLM | Industry standards |

on UNIX systems. Since NFS makes heavy demands on data throughput, a LAN with a suitably high bandwidth (for example, Ethernet) is an absolute prerequisite for sensible and transparent operation.

The fixed association with a protocol hierarchy is seen as being advantageous to interoperability, since experience indicates that greater flexibility only leads to manufacturers installing their own preferred protocol hierarchy, thus making it impossible to exchange data with other makes of computers. However, in the future, other combinations in the lower layer will be possible and desirable. With System V Release 4, the RPC layer has been made sufficiently flexible to support operations over other transport protocols.

# Remote Procedure Call

*Remote Procedure Call* (RPC) is a session layer protocol. It was especially developed for NFS, but is used in many networked applications. RPC is specified in RFC 1050 (Sun Microsystems, 1988) and also in the documentation delivered with NFS systems or products.

RPC forms the basis for message exchange in all NFS applications. RPC may be used in the design and development of network services, which, as the name indicates, are used in a similar way to subroutine calls or *procedures* in high-level programming languages. This mode of working eases the programmer's tasks in the design and implementation of distributed programs. The source code for RPC (and for the *External Data Representation* (XDR)) is available free of charge from Sun.

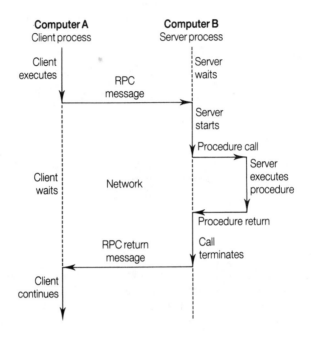

**Figure 9.2**   Execution of an RPC.

## Mode of operation

The method of working is similar to the local procedure call. In the case of a local procedure call, the parameters are assigned to the calling procedure at a specific point (for example, the stack). The program then branches into the subprocedure which carries out its work and returns. The results of the subprocedure can only be received by the calling procedure.

The execution of an RPC consists of the following steps (see Figure 9.2):

(1) Activation by the client program. The request parameters are packed into a data packet.

(2) Sending of the request and unpacking of the parameters in the server program.

(3) Execution of the request (the procedure) in the server.

(4) Packing and returning of the results to the client.

(5) Unpacking of the results by the client and continuation of the normal program execution.

Table **9.2**   Specification of the program-number area.

| Beginning | End | Use |
|---|---|---|
| 0 | 1FFFFFFF | Sun |
| 20000000 | 3FFFFFFF | Free for developers |
| 40000000 | 5FFFFFFF | Transient programs |
| 60000000 | 7FFFFFFF | Reserved |
| 80000000 | 9FFFFFFF | Reserved |
| A0000000 | BFFFFFFF | Reserved |
| C0000000 | DFFFFFFF | Reserved |
| E0000000 | FFFFFFFF | Reserved |

The packing and unpacking of the parameters and the results, the creation of a full RPC protocol header and the sending and receiving of the message are executed by library routines linked into the program.

## RPC protocol header

The RPC protocol is the chassis for transporting requests to the server, where they flow into *procedures*. The programmer can define an arbitrary number of procedures between the client and the server, with arbitrary optional parameters and results.   A functionally coherent group of procedures is called a *service* in RPC jargon. Each service is assigned a so-called *program number*, which is well-defined since usually *only one* service is provided by *one* server program. When, in NFS discussions, we talk of *user protocols*, it is these RPC programs which we have in mind, since the definition of a service represents a protocol. The NFS protocol is itself such a group of RPC procedures.

As can be seen from the protocol header of a request packet in Figure 9.3, a packet contains the following items defining a request:

- a program number
- a procedure number
- a version number.

The server uses these entries to branch into the correct subprocedure. All the fields of the RPC protocol header are coded in the XDR format.

Sun has defined the conventions outlined in Table 9.2 for the allocation of the program number.

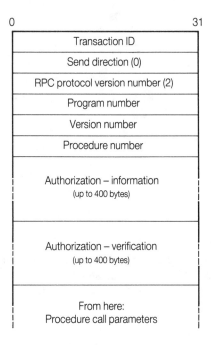

**Figure 9.3** RPC protocol header.

The individual procedures of a program are usually numbered sequentially. The version number allows several versions of a procedure to be supported within a server; if there is no procedure with the given version number, the request is rejected. By convention, procedure 0 of each program is used for test purposes: it contains a null routine, which returns immediately supplying a void result. Thus, it is very easy to test RPC servers for signs of life.

The transaction ID identifies the particular request. Since it is returned in the response, the client may use it to allocate incoming messages to that request. Servers recognize from the transaction ID whether a request is repeated by the client. Transaction IDs need not necessarily be increasing, they must simply be different from request to request. Like the transaction ID, the field for entry of the send direction is contained in every RPC message; it contains the value 0 in the RPC call and 1 in the response.

## Authentication

An RPC message must sometimes also contain information with which the client authenticates itself to the server. The server must be able to check the validity of this authentication information. The areas provided for this follow directly after the procedure definitions or the return status entry in the protocol header. This enables servers to restrict access to services (such as the reading of specific information) to authorized clients. The authentication information consists of two parts: the information itself and a *verifier*. Clients may use these two parts to determine whether the response returned is actually authentic – that it comes from the desired server. RPC itself does not specify how the authentication should be carried out; it only makes an area of up to 400 bytes available for the relevant information. At the beginning of each area is a label which specifies the type and length of the authentication information. From this label, the recipient of the message can determine the structure of the information (and evaluate it accordingly). The mechanism caters for any type of authentication information. Currently, the following types are predefined:

- AUTH_NONE: No authentication information; both parts of following area have length 0. AUTH_NONE is used when it is not required to check the authorization.

- AUTH_UNIX: UNIX access rights based on user and group IDs to be entered by the client. This type is used in the NFS protocol. AUTH_UNIX information is not accompanied by a verifier, the area provided for this is occupied by AUTH_NONE.

- AUTH_SHORT: Short version of the authentication identification, generated and returned by the server. Usually, this is a reference to authentication information from a previous RPC request, already stored in the server.

- AUTH_DES: Authentication information in the form of a character string as data with a DES-encrypted time stamp as verifier. This type of identification information is used by *secure NFS*.

As the alert reader will immediately note, a file access system such as NFS which uses AUTH_UNIX for access protection cannot be secure. A clever programmer would be able to generate counterfeit NFS requests and so gain unauthorized file access. Secure NFS closes this security loophole. This variant may be obtained with SunOS Version 4.0 and System V Release 4.

## Dependence on the transport protocol

Since the RPC protocol is independent of the nature of the message transport, an RPC program may be executed over both TCP and UDP.

Some servers offer their services over both protocols and leave the choice to the client. However, the choice of the transport protocol leads to some semantic differences in the behaviour of RPC which must be taken into account when designing a user protocol.

As a rule, RPC is used with UDP, since the majority of RPC-based applications are transaction oriented. When UDP is used, the maximum size of the data section of an RPC packet is restricted since, for practical reasons, UDP packets cannot be arbitrarily large. There is no theoretical upper limit for TCP; therefore, if large data sets are to be sent, this protocol should be preferred.

Normally, it is assumed that data sets of up to 8 kbytes may be sent over UDP. In BSD systems with integrated NFS, this upper limit is used up by UDP packets with a maximum of 8800 bytes (8 kbytes data plus RPC/XDR additions); other systems are limited to 2048 bytes. When TCP is used, RPC messages are packed into blocks with a 4-byte length field; thus, theoretically, several billion bytes may be moved in a single RPC.

A common occurrence in the past, in System V TCP/IP implementations under STREAMS, has been that UDP packets of over 4096 bytes were truncated.

Since, when UDP is used, forwarding of a message in the transport layer is not guaranteed, the RPC layer must take charge of reliability here. This is provided using a timer in the client which retransmits the unanswered RPC message after a given time interval has elapsed. The duration of the timer and the permissible number of retransmissions may be altered by the client program.

However, the issuing of an alarm does not necessarily mean that the execution of a request has been prevented by an error. It is equally possible that the processing of the request in the server has been delayed or that the response packet has been lost. In the latter case, if the request in the server has already been executed, its retransmission after the alarm has terminated would start it up again. Thus, the user protocol design for UDP applications should ensure that a request with the same parameters always delivers the same result; thus, that it may be arbitrarily repeated. The best example of this is the NFS read request which always provides the exact file position and length; in this case, inadvertent repetition would only recover the same data again. This is another reason why NFS does not allow access to special files; many devices, for example, terminals, only operate serially and do not usually allow for repetitions. This repeatability is called *idempotence* in RPC jargon. Some servers attempt to improve performance here using the transaction ID in the RPC protocol header; in order to avoid surplus repeated requests, they check whether a request has already been seen and is now being or has just been processed.

When TCP is used, no retransmissions may be initiated at the RPC level since TCP itself retransmits the message until it reaches the server. In other words, the server receives the message either once only or not at all.

If message forwarding is unsuccessful, the RPC layer will be notified and may inform the application program. The same is also true for the RPC response message from the server.

Since data transmission with TCP is reliable, another mode of operation is available when required, batching. Batching involves the sending of RPC requests in rapid succession without waiting for the response to the previous call, for example, for the data-transmission phase of a file transfer implemented with RPC. This results in a considerably higher transfer rate between client and server, since the waiting times between request and response are omitted. To execute batching, client and server must have previously agreed that the server should not send response messages.

# External Data Representation

If we define the term 'protocol' to mean a declaration of the form of communication between two peers, then the External Data Representation (XDR) also falls into this category. As specified in RFC 1014 (Sun Microsystems, 1987), XDR is concerned with the definition of a format for data encoding. XDR does not have a protocol header or other protocol elements like other protocols. This declaration logically resides in the presentation layer.

## Background

The object of data communication is to exchange data between computers and operating systems of different origins and types. For a computer to understand data sent from another computer, the data must be presented in the same form or in a form agreed between the two computers, otherwise the recipient cannot convert the data into its own internal format. We have already come across this problem in our discussion of the TCP/IP protocol headers.

There are two modes of operation for the protocols of the presentation layer. In the *explicit format*, a description of the individual elements is transferred with the data, thus enabling the recipient to recover the structure of data records (as in ASN.1 *Basic Encoding Rules* (BER)). The *implicit format* involves an agreement between the two communication partners, prior to the data transfer, regarding the structure and presentation of the elements. XDR uses the implicit format.

## Data encoding

Different computer systems differ greatly as far as the representation of data is concerned. These differences may be determined by both hardware

Motorola 680x0, IBM 370, MIPS, SPARC

| Higher value | | | Lower value |
|---|---|---|---|
| Byte 1 | Byte 2 | Byte 3 | Byte 4 |

Intel 80x86, VAX, NS32000

| Lower value | | | Higher value |
|---|---|---|---|
| Byte 1 | Byte 2 | Byte 3 | Byte 4 |

**Figure 9.4** Big- and little-endian formats.

and software. In addition to the representation of integers and floating-point numbers, there are different ways of encoding text and complex data objects such as unions and structures.

Binary integer processing is used in all modern processor architectures. However, in the case of integers, the processor may store words consisting of several bytes in different ways, either with the least order byte (*little-endian*) at the lowest memory address or vice versa (*big-endian*).

Figure 9.4 makes the arrangement clear using a 32-bit word. Theoretically, the same difference could arise for the bit sequence within a byte, but in practice all processors use the big-endian format to arrange the bits in a byte.

Similarly, in the past, there were great differences in the representations of floating-point numbers. Table 9.3 shows the format defined in the IEEE standard 754-1985 (IEEE, 1985), which is today used in many standard processors and co-processors.

While the encoding of numerical values is usually determined by the processor hardware, the software is responsible for encoding text and complex data objects. Without a mapping from codes to characters, text is simply a (meaningless) sequence of bytes. Standardized mapping tables include the ASCII and EBCDIC codes. Regrettably, these have fundamentally different structures, for example, the letter 'A' is represented by $41_{(16)}$ in ASCII and by $C1_{(16)}$ in EBCDIC.

Unions and structures are complex data objects constructed from the basic data types described above; they are defined by the programmer or the compiler. While program declarations are in principle interchangeable, the most frequent problem on binary exchange of these objects is the different alignment of the elements they contain.

An optimal access to data structures in the main memory usually

**Table 9.3**   ANSI/IEEE 754-1985 floating-point number format.

| Function | Size |
|---|---|
| Mantissa | 23 bits |
| Exponent | 8 bits |
| Sign | 1 bit |

assumes that the individual elements lie on the processor word boundaries (thus, their start address is even and/or divisible by four). Most processors require an additional cycle for operations over word boundaries and some (for example, the 68010 processor) cannot work at all with unaligned addresses. Since elements within structures do not always have a length which is a multiple of the word size, most compilers cater for this with automatically inserted padding, so that, according to the system, consecutive elements begin at addresses divisible by two or four. The structure shown in Figure 9.5 (given in C notation) may consist of 7, 8 or 12 bytes on different systems. For all the areas shown, appropriate specifications must be determined by XDR.

## Specifications

The data elements converted into XDR format are sequentially written to the data buffer (serialized) and then sent. The conversion from XDR (decoding) into an internal, possibly different, format is the job of the receiving computer.

XDR uses a format of 8-bit bytes with a big-endian bit sequence. All integer data types (in C notation *char*, *short* and *long* together with the type *enum*) are converted to 4-byte integers in big-endian format. In addition to the defined C data types, there is a 64-bit integer *hyper* and a Boolean type *bool*, which are treated analogously. The IEEE format is used for floating-point numbers.

```
struct example {
    char c;  /* begins at position 0 */
    short s; /* begins at position 1, 2 or 4 */
    long l;  /* begins at position 3, 4 or 8 */
};
```

**Figure 9.5**   Example of a structure with various word boundaries.

The canonical format procedure used in XDR, in which, under certain circumstances, every value must be converted by the sender and reconverted by the receiver, is not uncontroversial. While there are no disadvantages for computers whose processors operate using the byte order specified by XDR, message traffic between computers with the little-endian format requires a double (totally unnecessary) conversion. It would, for example, be possible to send a label with the message which would permit the recipient to recognize the byte order and convert it only when necessary.

Byte sequences are, as before, sent as a sequence of bytes, padded to be a multiple of 4. For a variable-length sequence, a length field is used to enable the recipient to distinguish between data and padding. The same applies to arrays of structures or unions which XDR processes as byte sequences. Text is encoded in the ASCII format. Structure elements are aligned to 4-byte boundaries (here the requirement for a total length divisible by 4 is naturally met).

A special language, similar to C, has been developed to describe XDR data formats. This may be used to describe the data objects exchanged in the user protocols and to define RPC services. There is also a compiler which generates C programs from XDR definitions (see RPC/XDR programming in Chapter 11). XDR need not always be installed only with RPC or networks. Basically, for each data exchange, the systems must agree upon a common data format. The XDR language may then be used as a 'data dictionary', although as yet there are no language elements for bit fields, bitmaps or *Binary-Coded Decimal* (BCD) numbers.

## Packet structure

Now that we have discussed all the protocol layers from the cable to the application, the RPC packet structure shown in Figure 9.6 should be practically self-explanatory. (Clearly, this packet is intended for an Ethernet network with UDP as the transport protocol.) From the protocol headers, we can clearly determine the individual protocol layers which are involved in the communication.

## Port mapper

As outlined in the discussion of TCP/IP, a rendezvous between client and server processors is made by calling a server port number which must be known to the client. If this principle of a defined port number were also to be used for RPC programs (with the increase in computer networking, there may be thousands of these in the future), there would soon be a problem with the allocation of free port numbers, resulting in unsolvable conflicts.

**Packet start**

| |
|---|
| Ethernet header |
| IP header |
| UDP header |
| RPC header |
| User data in XDR format |
| Ethernet checksum |

**Packet end**

**Figure 9.6**  Structure of an Ethernet packet with RPC data.

Thus, the *port mapper*, which dynamically binds port numbers to RPC programs, was created for the RPC protocol.

## Mode of operation of the port mapper

The port mapper server operates like a directory service, which essentially controls a mapping table relating RPC programs and/or version numbers to the local UDP or TCP port numbers, at which a service (server) is available. The port mapper itself occupies port 111 in both TCP and UDP.

An RPC server is usually allocated a free port number by the system on program start-up. It then registers this number with the port mapper together with the parameters of the service it offers. When a client wishes to access an RPC service, it first sends an enquiry including the program, procedure and version numbers together with the type of the desired protocol to the port mapper of the target computer (the computer on which the procedure is to be executed). It receives the port number of the service by return and can then send the request directly to the server. Since the client caches the port number, it is not necessary to repeat the port mapper enquiry for other RPC requests. Since in the client the port numbers are not stored in a file but in main memory, a new enquiry cycle is needed at every system start.

**Table 9.4**   RPC protocol parameters for PORTMAP.

| Name | Value |
|------|-------|
| Program number | 100000 |
| Version number | 1 |
| Transport protocol | TCP, UDP |

In addition to its many advantages, this dynamic mapping also has the disadvantage that if the port mapper breaks down the RPC service cannot then be obtained.

## Port mapper protocol

Client and server both communicate with the port mapper via RPC procedures. The parameters of this protocol are shown in Table 9.4.

The RPC procedures defined in the port mapper protocol may be taken from Figure 9.7. It is not appropriate to give the exact description of the procedure parameters and the results at this point. The symbolic names used should provide a clear description of the corresponding functions. Further information may be found in the NFS documentation and in RFC 1050 (Sun Microsystems, 1988).

As Figure 9.7 shows, here too there is a procedure 0 which, by definition, does nothing, has no parameters and returns a void value. The procedures PMAPPROC_SET and PMAPPROC_UNSET are used by the server to register or (respectively) de-register a service. PMAPPROC_GETPORT and PMAPPROC_DUMP supply an individual port number or the complete port mapper table. A client may use the procedure PMAPPROC_CALLIT to broadcast an RPC message to all existing servers (in the network) of a given service.

## Client server mapping

One of the greatest disadvantages of the current RPC implementation is the fact that a client must know exactly on which computer a given server is available. When the mapping of servers and computers changes, manual intervention is generally required on the client side.

It would be desirable to have a service which would search for a server on behalf of the client, such as, for example, the *Location Broker* of the Hewlett-Packard/Apollo *Network Computing System* (NCS). In OSF's DCE RPC, this service is provided by the name service. YPBIND could provide a similar service for NFS systems, but regrettably it is not used for that purpose.

```
/*
 * Procedure 0, Does nothing:
 */
0. PMAPPROC_NULL ()
        returns ()

/*
 * Procedure 1, Sets an entry:
 */
1. PMAPPROC_SET (prog, vers, prot, port)
                        returns (success)

/*
 * Procedure 2, Deletes an entry:
 */
2. PMAPPROC_UNSET (prog, vers, dummy1, dummy2)
                         returns (success)

/*
 * Procedure 3, Searches for an entry:
 */
3. PMAPPROC_GETPORT (prog, vers, prot, dummy)
                            returns (port)

/*
 * Procedure 4, Transfers the whole table:
 */
4. PMAPPROC_DUMP ()
  returns (maplist)

/*
 * Procedure 5, Indirect broadcast:
 */
5. PMAPPROC_CALLIT (prog, vers, proc, args)
                      returns (port, results)
```

**Figure 9.7**   Port mapper protocol.

# Network File System protocol

The NFS protocol (Sun Microsystems, 1989) consists of a number of RPC procedures, constructed on the same principle as the port mapper protocol.

**Table 9.5**   RPC protocol parameters for NFS.

| Name | Value |
|------|-------|
| Program number | 100003 |
| Version number | 2 |
| Transport protocol | UDP |
| Port number | 2049 |

Table 9.5 shows the constants of the NFS service. The current version of the NFS protocol is number 2; version 1 was never issued.

The specification of port number 2049 is surprising. However, as noted earlier, port numbers may be arbitrarily chosen and the mapping between services and port numbers is made by the port mapper! The explanation is simple; this number is a relict from the past which has been retained, at least until the next version of NFS. This port number was accidentally set to 2049 as a result of negligence in the implementation and, once its removal had been neglected at the start, later correction was impossible for reasons of upward compatibility.

## Specifications of RPC services

RPC services, like the NFS protocol, are best specified using the XDR language, whose elements we have not yet discussed. One advantage of this language is the fact that RPC/XDR definitions may be converted into C programs using the compiler *rpcgen*. These C programs may be routines to convert the parameters into XDR format or frameworks for RPC server programs which must only be extended by implementation of the services themselves. You will find more about these functions in Chapter 11 on RPC/XDR programming.

A formal definition of the XDR language at this point would be rather dry and of little help. Instead, we shall introduce the NFS protocol using a somewhat simpler and clearer representation which is also found in the NFS manuals (in which the specifications are usually given). The simplified representation provides a splendid explanation of the similarity between RPC and local procedures and to a large extent agrees with the syntax of the XDR language.

As in the representation of the port mapper protocol, a procedure with its parameters and return values is represented in the following form:

```
<Procedure number>.<Procedure name> (<Parameter>)
                              returns (<Results>)
    <Declaration of the arguments>
    <Declaration of the results>
```

Before we consider the NFS procedures individually, we must take a more detailed look at some of the data objects and structures which they use.

## Discriminated unions

In the XDR language, the term *discriminated union* stands for a labelled area which may contain various data objects.  The label provides information about the type of the data object.  The data area of a discriminated union also begins physically with a label followed by the data itself. It is interesting that explicit formats, avoided in the XDR protocol, are here reintroduced through the back door. In the XDR language, such an object is represented as shown in the following example:

```
union switch (status) {
    ERROR:
      int errorcode;
    OK:
      string text<MAXDATA>;
    default:
      struct {}
  } result;
```

The object *result* begins with a label *status* which may take the values *ERROR* or *OK*. This is followed by either a field *errorcode* or a character string *text*. Every other value denotes an empty set.

The entry in pointed brackets *<MAXDATA>* indicates that *text* is a variable-length character string, where the value of *MAXDATA* is the maximum length. Fixed-length objects are denoted by square brackets, as in [*MAXDATA*]. These length entries are also used in other array definitions.

Discriminated unions are (as our example demonstrates) often used as results of procedures: an error code is returned in the case of an error; data is returned in the case of success. In programming local subprocedures in C, in such a case, one would return a pointer to the data, which would have value 0 in the case of error. When computer boundaries are crossed, this method cannot be used, since, unlike local calls where cross-references to data may be given as parameters, in the RPC context the data itself must always be exported. (This difference should always be noted when defining RPC procedures.)

## NFS protocol constants

The following constants are defined for the NFS protocol:

```
/*
 * The maximum number of bytes in a READ or
 * WRITE request
```

```
*/
const MAXDATA = 8192; /* const defines a constant */

/*
 * The maximum number of bytes in a path name
 */
const MAXPATHLEN = 1024;

/*
 * The maximum number of bytes in a path name component
 */
const MAXNAMLEN = 255;

/*
 * Size of the file entry pointer 'cookie'
 * returned by READDIR
 */
const COOKIESIZE = 4;

/*
 * Size of a file handle
 */
const FHSIZE = 32;
```

## NFS data types

The most important data object in the NFS protocol is the *file handle* (*fhandle*). This contains entries which uniquely identify a file on the NFS server. File handles are given as parameters in all NFS procedures and are references to the files with which the operation itself should be executed. They are thus very similar to the file descriptor in standard UNIX system calls. Since the NFS protocol must be valid for various systems, the file handle is defined to be a 32-byte (FHSIZE) format-free data field or so-called *opaque* object. Its contents are generated by the NFS server as a result of various RPC procedures and can only be understood by the server (in other words, the client receives the handle and sends it on every operation with the file; it cannot and should not manipulate it). The definition of this object is also unformatted:

```
typedef opaque fhandle[FHSIZE];
```

File handles are delivered to the client as a result of the procedures LOOKUP, CREATE and MKDIR.

Naturally, we know the information which the server usually stores in the file handle in UNIX systems:

- The *major/minor device number* of the device driver of the file system containing the file.
- The *index node (inode) number* of the file addressed.
- A local inode generation number which fixes the instance of the inode.

These entries are sufficient to enable the NFS server to recognize a file uniquely. We shall go into the function of the generation number in more depth in our discussion of the weaknesses of the NFS protocol.

In some calls, path names and file names are given, which are defined as follows:

```
typedef string path<MAXPATHLEN>;
typedef string filename<MAXNAMLEN>;
```

The results of NFS procedures may take the following values:

```
typedef enum {
    NFS_OK = 0,
    NFSERR_PERM = 1,
    NFSERR_NOENT = 2,
    NFSERR_IO = 5,
    NFSERR_NXIO = 6,
    NFSERR_ACCES = 13,
    NFSERR_EXIST = 17,
    NFSERR_NODEV = 19,
    NFSERR_NOTDIR = 20,
    NFSERR_ISDIR = 21,
    NFSERR_FBIG = 27,
    NFSERR_NOSPC = 28,
    NFSERR_ROFS = 30,
    NFSERR_NAMETOOLONG = 63,
    NFSERR_NOTEMPTY = 66,
    NFSERR_DQUOT = 69,
    NFSERR_STALE = 70,
    NFSERR_WFLUSH = 99
} stat;
```

Most of these definitions are well known to UNIX programmers; they correspond to the error codes defined in */usr/include/sys/errno.h*.

Only two values are new. NFS_OK stands for the successful execution of a procedure. NFSERR_STALE stands for invalid (stale) file handle. The error code NFSERR_WFLUSH is not currently used.

*ftype* ('file type') defines the file types known in NFS. Here, the similarities to UNIX situations are not purely coincidental:

```
typedef enum {
    NFNON = 0, /* no file */
    NFREG = 1, /* regular file */
    NFDIR = 2, /* directory */
    NFBLK = 3, /* block-oriented file */
    NFCHR = 4, /* character-oriented file */
    NFLNK = 5  /* symbolic link */
} ftype;
```

No other data types are defined. System V FIFOs (which are also known as named pipes) are not stand-alone file types in NFS Version 2, since they do not exist on BSD systems (and thus neither do they exist on the earlier SunOS versions). They may be emulated by a combination of invalid entries in other fields and should be included in a later NFS protocol version.

The structure *fattr* ('file attributes') defines the attributes of a file as far as they are important to the NFS client. Elements of *fattr* include time stamps, for which there is an individual type definition, *timeval*:

```
typedef struct {
    unsigned seconds;    /* seconds */
    unsigned useconds;   /* microseconds */
} timeval;

typedef struct {
    ftype    type;       /* file type */
    unsigned mode;       /* access rights */
    unsigned nlink;      /* number of links */
    unsigned uid;        /* owner's user ID */
    unsigned gid;        /* owner's group ID */
    unsigned size;       /* size in bytes */
    unsigned blocksize;  /* size of a file block */
    unsigned rdev;       /* major and minor device */
    unsigned blocks;     /* size in blocks */
    unsigned fsid;       /* file system ID */
    unsigned fileid;     /* catalogue number */
    timeval  atime;      /* time of last access */
    timeval  mtime;      /* time of last modification */
```

```
    timeval  ctime;      /* time of installation */
  } fattr;
```

UNIX specialists will immediately recognize the similarity with the contents of the structure declared in */usr/include/sys/stat.h*, which is here only extended by a few entries.

The *sattr* ('set attributes') structure contains those attributes which may be set by system calls.

```
    typedef struct {
        unsigned mode;   /* access rights */
        unsigned uid;    /* user ID */
        unsigned gid;    /* group ID */
        unsigned size;   /* size */
        timeval  atime;  /* time of last access */
        timeval  mtime;  /* time of last modification */
      } sattr;
```

The discriminated union *attrstat* ('attributes and status') is supplied as a result in almost all NFS procedures. In the case of success, it contains the attributes of the altered file, otherwise it contains the error code defined by *stat*:

```
    typedef union switch (stat status) {
        NFS_OK:
            fattr    attributes;
        default:  struct {}
      } attrstat;
```

*diropargs* ('directory operation arguments') and *diropres* ('operation results') contain the arguments and results of operations with file directories:

```
    typedef struct {
        fhandle  dir;
        filename name;
      } diropargs;

    typedef union switch (stat status) {
        NFS_OK
            struct {
                fhandle file;
                fattr    attributes;
            }
        default:
```

```
                    struct {}
            } diropres;
```

## NFS protocol specification

In this section, the NFS procedures of the NFS protocol are presented and discussed in detail.

### Null

```
        0.  NFSPROC_NULL () returns ()
```

Like all other RPC services, the NFS protocol begins with the procedure 0, which does not contain any arguments and returns a void result.

### Fetch file attributes

```
        1.  NFSPROC_GETATTR (file) returns (reply)
            fhandle  file;
            attrstat reply;
```

This procedure returns the attributes of the file specified in the file handle, for example, as a result of the UNIX system calls *access, open, stat* and *fstat*. File attributes are held in the NFS client in a cache, so that this frequently used information is always ready. Entries in the cache are time stamped. If the difference between the time of the time stamp entry and the actual time is greater than three seconds for files or 30 seconds for directories the information is fetched again from the server. Thus, it is possible that alterations to file directories through a second client only appear after this time interval has elapsed.

### Set file attributes

```
        2.  NFSPROC_SETATTR (file, attributes) returns (reply)
            fhandle  file;
            sattr    attributes;
            attrstat reply;
```

This procedure is used to set attributes, for example, via the UNIX system calls *chown, fchown, chmod, fchmod, truncate, ftruncate* and *utime*. The altered attributes are returned as a result.

*Read file system root*

```
3.  NFSPROC_ROOT () returns ()
```

This procedure is obsolete and is not used.

*Look up file name*

```
4.  NFSPROC_LOOKUP (which) returns (reply)
        diropargs which;
        diropres  reply;
```

LOOKUP supplies the client with a file handle corresponding to a file name in a specified directory (*which*), thus making the subsequent operations with the file or the directory possible. The client uses this procedure to find its way around in the file system of another computer or NFS server.

The client uses LOOKUP to conduct a step-by-step search through path names given to it in a program and, in certain circumstances, may even call an individual RPC procedure for every path name component. This procedure is best explained with an example.

Let us assume that a server file system is locally mounted in the directory */nfs*. In order to find a file handle for the file */nfs/a/b/c/file*, the client system first searches the file system root / for the directory *nfs* whose attributes it has stored locally. In so doing, it determines that *nfs* is the mounting point of an NFS file system and now uses LOOKUP to search for the file handle for the directory *a* on the server. Then it searches for *b* in *a*, and so on, until it finally finds the file handle for *file*.

Why does the client not simply send the last part of the file name (*a/b/c/file*) to the server, leaving the server to return the file handle for *file* and thus saving time and system resources? Let us see what would happen if we used this method with path names such as */nfs/a/b/../../tmp/file*. In this case, in the NFS server data tree, */nfs/a/b* is switched backwards twice by .. , and in fact the file */tmp/file* is located on the client computer. In other words, this method of path name evaluation would create insoluble problems for the server.

UNIX path names of this type are however completely legal. Of course, they are not generated by a user, but by shell procedures or programs. Thus, we have shown that the step-by-step search for a path name using the LOOKUP procedure is the best solution. The time spent searching for path names may be shortened if the client uses a directory cache. The file handles for directories which are frequently searched will be stored in this cache; thus, there is little or no loss of performance.

### Read the contents of a symbolic link

```
5.  NFSPROC_READLINK (file) returns (reply)
        fhandle file;
        union switch (stat status) {
           NFS_OK:
               path    data;
           default:
               struct {}
        } reply;
```

BSD systems define symbolic links or files which contain the path name of another file instead of data and are thus pointers to other files. If the system recognizes a symbolic link file, the pointer is read by the system even under NFS. It is then evaluated and the specified file is addressed. Up to five embedded symbolic links may be used. In order that programs such as the command *ls* may also evaluate symbolic link files, there is a system call named *readlink*. The RPC procedure NFSPROC_READLINK allows access to symbolic links over NFS.

### Read a file

```
6.  NFSPROC_READ (file, offset, count, totalcount)
   returns (reply)
        fhandle  file;
        unsigned offset;
        unsigned count;
        unsigned totalcount;
        union switch (stat status) {
           NFS_OK:
               fattr   attributes;
               string data<MAXDATA>;
           default:
               struct {}
        } reply;
```

With this procedure, which is activated following a *read* or *exec* system call, the NFS client reads from a file belonging to the server; the latter, for its part, returns data and file attributes. *offset* explicitly sets the file read counter in the server at each call. The parameter *totalcount* is unused.

### Write to cache

```
7.  NFSPROC_WRITECACHE () returns ()
```

This procedure is not used in the current version of NFS.

## Write to file

```
8.  NFSPROC_WRITE (file, beginoffset, offset,
    totalcount, data) returns (reply)
        fhandle  file;
        unsigned beginoffset;
        unsigned offset;
        unsigned totalcount;
        string   data<MAXDATA>;
        attrstat reply;
```

This procedure, which is activated following a *write* system call, is used by
the NFS client to write to a file belonging to the server. The parameters
*totalcount* and *beginoffset* are unused. The length of the data to be
written is given in the length field of the *data* area.

## Create file

```
9.  NFSPROC_CREATE (where, attributes) returns (dir)
        diropargs where;
        sattr      attributes;
        diropres  dir;
```

CREATE, which is activated by the system calls *creat*, *mknod* and *open*,
generates new files in the server. The result of this call is the file handle for
the new file.

## Delete file

```
10.  NFSPROC_REMOVE (which) returns (status)
        diropargs which;
        stat      status;
```

This procedure, which is activated by the system call *unlink*, deletes files
on the server.

## Rename file

```
11.  NFSPROC_RENAME (from, to) returns (status)
        diropargs from;
        diropargs to;
        stat      status;
```

NFSPROC_RENAME supports the atomic renaming of a file or directory, for example, in the system call *rename*.

### Generate link

```
12.  NFSPROC_LINK (from, to) returns (status)
         fhandle  from;
         diropargs to;
         stat      status;
```

This is activated by the system call *link*. It generates a so-called hard link (another directory entry for a file) within a file system.

### Generate symbolic link

```
13.  NFSPROC_SYMLINK (from, to, attributes)
     returns (status)
         diropargs from;
         path      to;
         sattr     attributes;
         stat      status;
```

This procedure is activated by the system call *symlink* and generates a symbolic link.

### Create directory

```
14.  NFSPROC_MKDIR (where, attributes) returns (reply)
         diropargs where;
         sattr     attributes;
         diropres  reply;
```

This procedure is activated by the system call *mkdir* and generates an empty directory with the entries . and .. (where .. denotes the directory above in the file system tree).

### Delete directory

```
15.  NFSPROC_RMDIR (which) returns (status)
         diropargs which;
         stat      status;
```

This procedure is activated by the system call *rmdir* and deletes a directory.

The system calls *rmdir* and *mkdir* were not available in the first versions
of System V (System V.2 and earlier); thus, for upward compatibility with
older systems they are emulated by some client systems.

## Read directory

```
16.  NFSPROC_READDIR (dir, cookie, count)
   returns (entries)
       fhandle  dir;
       opaque   cookie[COOKIESIZE];
       unsigned count;
       union switch (stat, status) {
           NFS_OK:
               typedef union switch (boolean valid) {
                   TRUE:
                     struct {
                         unsigned fileid;
                         filename name;
                         opaque   cookie[COOKIESIZE];
                         entry    nextentry;
                     }
                   FALSE:
                     struct {}
               } entry;
               boolean eof;
               default:
       } entries;
```

The result of this procedure is a list of directory entries, each of which
consists of a file name, the inode number and the so-called 'cookie'. A
'cookie' is a pointer to a position in the directory.

Before giving further details of the parameters and results of
READDIR, we should ask why it is actually needed. Why is it not possible
to read the contents of a directory just as we would a file? The explanation
for this is simple and enlightening. Every operating system has its own
physical file system structure and its own directory format; they are not
even fully compatible between different UNIX derivatives. Only now are
UNIX systems being supplied which support several fixed-disk file systems
at once (for example, System V.3.2 with UNIX, MS-DOS and XENIX).
Since NFS is also required to function in a heterogeneous environment,
there is a specific format for the exchange of directory information. More
recent versions of UNIX (System V.3 or BSD versions with NFS) contain
generic system calls to read from directories (*getdents* or *getdirentries*).
However, the UNIX programmer never uses these calls directly, but always

through functions, such as *readdir*, supplied in the *directory* library routines. Attempts to read a directory over NFS using READ are rejected by the server with an error. However, for upward compatibility with old programs, some UNIX systems convert standard directory read operations within the NFS client to READDIR calls. Under certain circumstances, this may harm performance, for example, when accessing a directory randomly. Other server operating systems do not have directories similar to UNIX; in this case, emulation must take place in the server.

The format of the results of the READDIR procedure shows many similarities to UNIX, for example, the field *fileid* contains the inode number used in UNIX. The use of 'cookie' certainly needs to be explained. Since it is possible that, because of its size, a directory may not be contained in a single RPC message, it must be readable in sequential steps. The cookie is used to mark the position reached. In UNIX, the cookie is a file position; in other systems, it may be an index key. Because of these differences, the client cannot and should not evaluate the contents of the cookie. This data is, like a file handle, declared to be *opaque*.

The rather complicated results structure is the XDR version of a chained list, where the switch *valid* shows whether another directory entry follows (thus, it acts like a NULL pointer in C). *eof* tells us whether the end of the directory has been reached.

### Read file system attributes

```
17.  NFSPROC_STATFS (file) returns (reply)
        fhandle file;
        union switch (stat status) {
            NFS_OK:
                struct {
                    unsigned tsize;
                    unsigned bsize;
                    unsigned blocks;
                    unsigned bfree;
                    unsigned bavail;
                } fsattr;
            default:
                struct {}
        } reply;
```

This procedure returns information about the mounted file system, the number of blocks present (*blocks*), whether they are available (*bavail*) or free (*bfree*) and their sizes (*bsize*), together with the optimal transfer size (*tsize*) for READ and WRITE requests, etc. STATFS is executed, for example, by calling the UNIX command *df*. Regrettably, the number of free

inodes in the file system is not returned; thus, this value in the output of
*df* is always 0. STATFS is activated by the system call *ustat* in System V
or by *statfs* in BSD NFS systems.

## Particular features of the NFS protocol

The designers of NFS were interested in designing a very robust file access
service which, above all, would eradicate the painful problem of restart
after a failure of the server or client computer. The solution was a *stateless*
protocol, in which the server did not have to store any information about
the current state or the progress of the dialogue with the client (for example,
whether or not a file was opened or closed). Thus, the NFS protocol does
not have the usual open and close operations. Unlike in standard UNIX
I/O routines, the read and write positions are always supplied to the server
on application.

   Since the *fhandle* for a file must always be unambiguous, it is
now possible, after a server failure and a subsequent restart, to continue
a read operation transparently, as far as the client program is concerned.
While the server is not available, the client system retransmits the read
request with the same parameters to the server at regular intervals, until
the server responds. This behaviour is particularly advantageous for diskless
workstations which cannot execute a meaningful function without the
server.

   The repeated issuing of requests when there is no answer is a
component part of the RPC mechanism. The waiting time between
the repeats (which increases exponentially according to the number of
unsuccessful attempts) and the number of repeats before total cut-off may
be parameterized using the command *mount*.

   The semantics of RPC procedures have to be defined in such a way
that repetition is not a problem. However, in the NFS protocol, in some
procedures (REMOVE, CREATE, RMDIR, MKDIR, LINK, SYMLINK and
SETATTR), this is not the case. Thus, for example, a file delete may not
be arbitrarily repeated (since after the first call the file is no longer present,
a second call would return an error message of the form 'File does not
exist'). Since NFS cannot be 100% protected against either overloaded
servers with high response times or lost response packets, here too we
must also reckon with redundant RPCs. So that these calls do not cause
problems, the NFS server implementation under UNIX uses a cache to log
previously terminated calls of all non-repeatable procedures together with
their transaction ID. The cache is used to recognize repeats of such requests
from RPC transaction IDs already stored in the cache; a positive response
is now returned in place of an error code. Attempts have been made to
extend this cache to WRITE procedures (Juszczak, 1989), to decrease the
server load due to redundant repeated write operations.

   There is one other situation in which the stateless NFS protocol is not always an advantage, for example, in mapping the UNIX semantics over NFS. We shall discuss this problem and its solution in the next chapter on the implementation of NFS.

# MOUNT protocol

As we have seen, files are allocated and accessed in NFS servers by mounting a file tree on the server computer into the local file tree of the client computer. Then, the files of this tree may be accessed using the normal resources (system calls, programs). However, the NFS protocol is a protocol for file *access*, and thus it itself does not define procedures to activate the mounting process.

The file system mounting procedure should be viewed as a totally separate problem which is solved using the MOUNT protocol specified in RFC 1094 (Sun Microsystems, 1989).

## Background

The only information that an NFS client requires initially for access to a remote file system is the file handle of a directory, for example, a file system root. From this point on, the client may penetrate more deeply into the file system on its own, using the procedure NFSPROC_LOOKUP. The job of the MOUNT protocol is now to provide this file handle in the first place. The name of the file system will be given in the call.

In addition, the MOUNT protocol also contains other procedures, for example, to interrogate the so-called export list of the file systems available via NFS and MOUNT. Another task is to record the mounts between clients and servers, since knowledge of these considerably simplifies network management. This is taken care of by *mountd* (the server for the MOUNT protocol), which notes the computer and path names for every mounting procedure. Because of this division between mounting and file access, there is no feedback to the NFS server after the mounting procedure. All operations in the MOUNT protocol involve only the MOUNT server. The NFS client may access the server so long as it is in possession of a valid file handle (here it does not matter if the MOUNT server has altered its tables in the meantime).

## Specification of the MOUNT protocol

The procedure DUMP (see Figure 9.8) provides a list of the file systems on the server which are currently mounted on the client computer. The procedure EXPORT provides a list of the exported file systems. UMNT and UMNTALL delete one or all (respectively) of the entries of a client in the corresponding server. We again note that there is no guarantee that

```
0.   MNTPROC_NULL () returns ()

1.   MNTPROC_MNT (directory) returns (reply)
         dirpath  dirname;
         fhstatus reply;

2.   MNTPROC_DUMP () returns (mountlist)
         union switch (boolean more_entries) {
             TRUE:
                 struct {
                     name       hostname;
                     dirpath    directory;
                     mountlist nextentry;
                 }
             FALSE:
                 struct {}
         } mountlist;

3.   MNTPROC_UMNT (directory) returns ()
         dirpath directory;

4.   MNTPROC_UMNTALL () returns ()

5.   MNTPROC_EXPORT () returns (exportlist)
         union switch (boolean more_entries) {
             TRUE:
                 struct {
                     dirpath        filesys;
                     typedef union switch (boolean more_groups) {
                         TRUE:
                             struct {
                                 name    grname;
                                 groups nextgroup;
                             }
                         FALSE:
                             struct {}
                     } groups;
                     mountlist nextentry;
                 }
             FALSE:
                 struct {}
         } exportlist;
```

**Figure 9.8**   MOUNT protocol.

**Table 9.6**   RPC protocol parameters for MOUNT.

| Parameter | Value |
|-----------|-------|
| Program number | 100005 |
| Version number | 1 |
| Transport protocol | UDP |

the *mountd* information agrees with those NFS client–server relationships which are actually active (this is particularly the case if the client computer has crashed). For this reason, an UMNTALL call to generally delete all existing entries on all MOUNT servers is usually broadcast when the client computer starts up. You will find more about this in the discussion of the *mount* and *umount* commands in the next chapter.

The result produced by the MNT procedure has the following structure:

```
typedef union switch (unsigned status) {
    0:
        fhandle directory;
    default:
        struct {}
} fhstatus;
```

Table 9.6 lists the parameters of the MOUNT protocol.

# Network Information Service

The Yellow Pages (YP) protocol, like the NFS, MOUNT or port mapper protocols, is an RPC service of the application layer. As the name Yellow Pages indicates, YP provides a directory service. YP has recently been renamed Network Information Service (NIS), since the name Yellow Pages is a registered trademark. We shall continue to use YP in this book, since it is the name by which the service is most commonly known.

As we mentioned in the section on RPC, the RPC authentication variant AUTH_UNIX is based on the same numerical user and group IDs used in the UNIX system. Thus, a prerequisite for the orderly granting of an access right is that the NFS client and server have identical mappings from the user ID to the user name. Assignment of the user ID is as a rule particularly critical; it is mapped to the user name on UNIX systems via the file */etc/passwd*. Since each UNIX system in the network manages its own */etc/passwd* file, we must reckon with overlaps, resulting in the

**Table 9.7**  Overlapping user IDs in different computers.

| Computer | User ID | User name |
|----------|---------|-----------|
| work | santi | 123 |
| home | christa | 123 |

mapping of a single user ID to two different user names on different systems. If the specification in Table 9.7 were in force and the processor *work* also had access over NFS to *home*, then the user *santi* could access files belonging to the user *christa*. The reverse would also be possible.

The YP protocol and the implementation of the YP service over server and client offers the possibility of managing the mappings in a central location in the network (the master server), thereby attempting to rule out overlaps of the user IDs. However, as before, programs running on other computers must have access over YP to the information held centrally. This is catered for by client functions in the form of YP library routines and some YP utilities.

It is possible to use a service such as YP for information other than the distribution of user and group IDs. Fortunately, this service is flexible and the network administrator may also use it for any other tables.

## Mode of operation

YP is a distributed system: it operates with several servers on different inter-communicating computers in the network. One of the servers is designated as master server by the network administrator; the master server possesses the original version of a table. In order to be fail-safe, and possibly to spread the load, other slave servers are started up on other computers. If the contents of the tables are altered, the slave servers are brought up to date with the latest version by the master server.

The information in the servers is organized in *maps*, which are each valid only within an administrative area (or *domain*). Thus, it is possible to distinguish between several domains in the same network, for example, different departments within a company. Since there is no feedback between the DNS and YP systems, the YP domains are not necessarily identical with the DNS domains and may actually be organized in a different way.

Every YP map contains data records consisting of an *index key* and the corresponding *information record* (usually an ASCII character string). To make this clearer, we shall consider an example from the */etc/passwd* file where the index is cleverly constructed from the user name. A query with the key *santi* would produce the data record:

```
santi:xjieQuhd:123:100:Michael Santifaller:/usr/santi:
```

**Table 9.8**   RPC protocol parameters for YP.

| Parameter | Value |
|---|---|
| Program number | 100004 |
| Version number | 1, 2 |
| Transport protocol | TCP, UDP |

As this example also shows, data records in the *passwd* map and in most other YP maps are in the same format as the corresponding line of the original file. This means that programs which previously accessed the */etc* files directly remain virtually unchanged. In addition to the */etc/passwd* and */etc/group* files needed to assign access rights in NFS operation, for technical administrative reasons, the following files are available on most NFS systems as YP maps:

- /etc/passwd
- /etc/group
- /etc/hosts
- /etc/ethers
- /etc/networks
- /etc/rpc
- /etc/services
- /etc/protocols
- /etc/netgroup
- /usr/lib/aliases.

In the case of some of the files, whose purposes we have already discussed a central management structure seems to be possible. The information in a file such as */etc/hosts* is equally valid for all computers in the network and YP guarantees that the latest version is available throughout the network. We shall discuss */etc/rpc, /etc/netgroup*, etc in the next chapter.

## YP procedures

The RPC identification for YP is as shown in Table 9.8. Naturally, there is a reason for the very surprising fact that an official service such as YP has two different and equally valid(!) version numbers. Since the first version of the protocol had serious design faults which led to problems on reconfiguration after a server crash, a second version had to be created very rapidly. For upward compatibility, both versions are supported by the server (which is possible using the version number in the RPC protocol).

The YP protocol incorporates procedures to search for YP servers in the network, to interrogate data records using a key, to transfer complete maps and to interrogate management information.

The YPBIND protocol, which we shall not discuss in detail here, is associated with the YP service. It helps the YP client to find a YP server in the network.

## Use of YP

Correctly used, there is no doubt that YP brings with it a simplification of NFS management. The installation and maintenance of a network-wide YP system is a task which always requires a certain amount of discipline. In particular, linking into the NFS operation on existing machines is comparatively demanding. Thus, many networks (particularly small ones) do not use YP at all. Since there is a tendency towards even larger networks, it is to be expected that management costs without the use of YP will one day no longer be tolerable. At the least, the problem of overlapping user IDs must be resolved in some way (possibly manually), since otherwise the security of NFS cannot be guaranteed.

Although the YP system has proved itself over many years, it is not uncontroversial, and rightly so. Its suitability as a general naming and authentication service (in some ways similar to DNS) is not only limited by its narrow reliance on UNIX specifics. Another factor is that the manner in which access rights are assigned in UNIX (and in the version of NFS described here) is insufficient for network operation. In addition, the implementation also includes a serious security loophole, which, for obvious reasons, we shall not discuss in further detail.

Better procedures, such as the Kerberos system (Miller *et al.*, 1987) or secure NFS, are already in use in some places. The OSF in its *Distributed Computing Environment* (DCE) offering has included Kerberos and a service called PasswdEtc, which provides programs with distributed access to information normally kept in */etc/passwd*. As previously mentioned, secure NFS is a component of the System V Release 4. It will be some time before these new services are widely available on all system platforms.

# 10

# Implementation of NFS

- NFS software packages

- Implementation of NFS under UNIX

- Mounting NFS file systems

- Diagnosis of RPC and NFS problems

- Lock manager

- Network Information Service

- NFS-based services

- NFS specialities

- NFS start-up, operation and management

- Remote file system organization

After our consideration in the previous chapter of the protocols used by NFS, we now turn our attention to the implementation of NFS on UNIX computers. Initially, we shall consider the embedding of the NFS server and client in more detail. Then follows a tour through NFS-specific and NFS-based programs and commands. At the end of the chapter, we look at some practical hints for putting NFS into operation.

# NFS software packages

## Reference versions

As we have already seen in earlier chapters, System V and BSD-based systems differ in respect of the functional environment implemented and the options of individual commands. Thus, it is now appropriate to name the version of NFS we have taken as our reference version; as an example of a network based on System V, we have used the NFS version for Interactive Systems 386/ix 2.0 (System V Release 3.2). This implementation comes from the firm Lachman Associates, which in the meantime has been bought out by Interactive. Most of the NFS products available on the market for System V Release 3 are based on the Lachman implementation. There are however other implementations for System V, for example, by the firm Wollongong.

On the BSD side, we had access to many different systems, including the DFS under SINIX V 5.2 on various Siemens MX computers, NFS under Ultrix on the DEC station 3100, and 4.2BSD with 3.2NFSSRC extensions on Digital Equipment's VAX. 3.2NFSSRC is the reference implementation of NFS for Sun and as such is the basis for most implementations, on both System V and BSD systems.

Naturally, the system variants include other manufacturer-specific restrictions or extensions which we shall not discuss in detail here – we are only concerned with the basic functions, which in all probability are available on all systems. Readers with a deeper interest are referred to the manufacturers' documentation in which all specific differences should be recognizable.

At this point, SunOS 4.0 deserves a brief mention. This version of the system introduced many new services, commands and options which to a large extent also appeared in System V Release 4. It will be some time before the new functionality, in whatever form, is taken up by other manufacturers. This book has, in part, attempted to describe these new functions; however, it has not provided a detailed treatment (at least at the current time) of those which are regarded to be too manufacturer specific.

## Directory conventions

In addition to differences in the options supported and in the functionality, there are also differences between the available systems as far as the location of commands is concerned. Regrettably, in System V, there are no particularly binding conventions as to where NFS commands are stored. As far as the following examples of screen dialogue are concerned, care has been taken to keep them as general as possible (and to mark deviations as such). If particular commands cannot be called directly on your system, the directories */etc* and */usr/etc* are probably the best starting points for a search. YP administrative commands are found in either */etc/yp* or */usr/etc/yp*. Note that on systems with System V or BSD universes, such as SINIX V.5 from Siemens, DYNIX from Sequent and Targon/35, the call must in certain circumstances be made in the ucb universe.

The directory */usr/etc* is used by Sun as an additional place in which to store system programs and data which are not required at the time the system is started; many of the NFS servers and commands are also located here. In our System V, from which most of our examples are taken, there is no such directory.

However, as networking increases, the usual conventions for system-specific directories on UNIX systems are increasingly obsolete. While one objective is that data and programs which are used by several systems in the network should only be stored once, there will always exist data which is only valid for a specific computer in the network (for example, a configuration file */etc/passwd*). Since not all computers in the network use the same processor, the distinction between the different architectures must be made. In SunOS 4.0 and System V Release 4, it was therefore decided to separate system programs, files and commands into general, computer- and architecture-specific directories, thereby generating a completely new directory hierarchy.

As far as the user of the system is concerned, this new distribution of files does not represent a visible alteration, since PATH variables and symbolic links render practically all these changes transparent. However, the network administrator must re-adapt himself in no uncertain way.

# Implementation of NFS under UNIX

## Embedding of the NFS client

One advantage of the implementation of NFS under UNIX is the transparent interface. A program does not notice whether it is accessing a file locally or over NFS. To achieve this, the corresponding system calls must be executed at a level external to the program in the UNIX operating system kernel. In other operating systems, this mechanism is known as a *redirector*, since it redirects normal system calls.

Access to files in operating systems consists of at least two complementary functions; firstly, the management of the file access (access control) on opening and closing files and, secondly, the actual allocation of storage medium data. In classical UNIX operating system kernels, the modules for the file access were amalgamated with the access control itself and there was no separation at all between the management and the 'insides' of the file system. For NFS operation, for example, UNIX had to be extended by functions to generate RPC requests to an NFS server.

In order to integrate the NFS client in an architecturally clean way, the Sun developers have provided a new internal system interface, the *Virtual File System* (VFS). VFS makes it possible to operate several different file systems in a system at the same time. The system I/O calls are in a higher layer which is independent of the file system. Access is managed in this layer before a lower (file-system dependent) layer is called.

Figure 10.1 shows the structure of the layers in the NFS UNIX kernel. Several file systems, such as UFS ('UNIX file system'), MS-DOS and NFS, may coexist below VFS.

VFS is used almost exclusively in BSD-based systems. In System V Version 3, AT&T implemented a similar concept, the File System Switch (FSS), for which an NFS variant is available. For future UNIX versions, the VFS interface has prevailed; it is of a higher level of abstraction and therefore more independent of the underlying file system. (In System V Release 4, FSS has already been replaced by VFS.)

Functionally, VFS is object oriented; the operating system kernel contains file system objects (files), directories, etc., represented in the form of *vnode* objects (vnode stands for virtual node). Every vnode is accompanied by references to the possible operations associated with this object. Thus, system calls such as *read* contain an additional step, namely, the evaluation of the vnode information and a jump to the corresponding file-specific routine. This routine carries out the steps needed to fetch the data, such as calling the disk controller or sending an RPC request, before finally handing the data over to the user program.

## Asynchronous I/O in the NFS client

In order to improve the data throughput, the data blocks in UNIX are held in a buffer, also termed a *buffer cache*. This mechanism is also used for data written or read via NFS. Usually, the physical I/O operation occurs asynchronously from the system call of a user program; the UNIX I/O system reads the next block of a file in advance (the data block should be in

Application programs

```
 ----------------------------------------------
|              System calls                    |
|----------------------------------------------|
|              VFS/FSS                         |
|----------------------------------------------|
|      |   M    |        |                     |
|      |   S    |        |                     |
|  U   |   -    |        |          N          |
|  F   |   D    |  ...   |          F           |
|  S   |   O    |        |          S          |
|      |   S    |        |                     |
|      |        |        |---------------------|
|      |        |        |        UDP          |
|   Device driver       |        IP           |
|                        |      network         |
 ----------------------------------------------
```

**Figure 10.1**  Embedding of NFS and other file systems in the UNIX kernel.

the buffer already) when requested by the user program. Conversely, data blocks are initially written to the buffer and later transferred to the diskwhen space is required in the buffer or on the next regular 'flush' of the buffer. These procedures are known as *read ahead* and *delayed write.*

In order to execute an RPC, such as those issued by NFS requests, a process context is required. This is made available in the UNIX operating system via the *biod* daemon, which supports read ahead and delayed write. *biod* improves the data throughput perceived by the NFS client, but is not absolutely necessary for operation. Without this daemon, there would be no asynchronous reads or writes over NFS. Usually, several *biod* processes (normally four) are active at the same time, thus enabling several operations to be executed in parallel. The program code executed by the *biod* process is stored in the operating system kernel and is activated by the system call *async_daemon().* Starting up too many *biod* daemons may in certain circumstances have undesirable consequences, namely, when through simultaneous delayed write of all the daemons the capacity of the UDP output buffer is exhausted. In this case, system performance is actually degraded.

Delayed write to a specific file is inhibited if a file is or has been locked by the lock manager: the blocks of this file are then sent immediately to the server and a so-called *write through* occurs.

## Embedding of the NFS server

As a process, the NFS server is logically located above the VFS interface and issues calls to the underlying file systems. In principle, it could be implemented under UNIX as an arbitrary RPC server like a normal user process. However, in order to obtain the greatest possible throughput, the NFS server in UNIX must be installed within the operating system kernel. In particular, this avoids the copying of data blocks between system and user address space.

In fact, the server process *nfsd* is started like a normal UNIX program when the NFS system is brought up. Immediately after opening the UDP port and registering with the port mapper, it executes the system call *nfs_svc()*, from which it only exits in the case of (involuntary) abnormal termination. As for *biod*, the server code itself is found in the operating system kernel. Although the NFS server registers itself with the port mapper, it always uses UDP port number 2049. Nowadays, NFS clients do not request the port number, but send RPC requests automatically to port 2049. This peculiarity is supported, for compatibility with earlier NFS versions, but it should be removed in the next version of the NFS protocol.

Like every other UNIX process, the NFS server must also remain inactive during a hard-disk read procedure and wait until the execution has been completed. During this time, other NFS requests for other clients may be processed. For this reason, several NFS servers (typically four) are simultaneously started up in order to serve a number of clients. The NFS servers take on requests from a common queue and process them sequentially.

## Supported access types

The NFS server only supports access to normal files and directories; while special files and named pipes (FIFOs) may be opened, they are interpreted and processed as resources on the local computer.

Named pipes and special files have one thing in common: the access method used for data exchange with them is not implemented in the file system itself; instead, the catalogue entry associated with the name entry in the file system only contains pointers to other modules such as device drivers in the UNIX operating system. For device drivers the *major device number* is an index in the device driver table. Equally, the data exchange between two computers over a named pipe does not involve storing and reading the data block in the 'named pipe' file on the disk, but uses the operating system data buffer. The NFS client never uses a file handle for these file types for a read or write operation, but simply evaluates the information contained in the file attributes. Thus, the floppy disk drive connected to the client computer is accessed by, for example, opening the file */dev/floppy* on the server. Two processes on different NFS client computers which open the same named pipe on an NFS server cannot communicate with one another over the pipe.

These restrictions are understandable when we consider the additional complications which would be associated with the operation of devices within the NFS protocol and the NFS implementation. A good example of this would be the need to support the system call *ioctl*, which almost exclusively involves data structures known only to the application program and the device driver, which thus cannot be converted by XDR. For communication between two processes, it is sensible to use a TCP connection rather than a named pipe. This is much more efficient than exchanging messages over an NFS server, which would also have to make provisions for flow control, etc.

For diskless workstations, the behaviour mode implemented in NFS is however sensible since the system must always be able to access its (own) peripherals.

## Restrictions on the operation of NFS

While NFS was designed to permit operation equivalent to the local file system, there are problems in marginal areas with the reproduction of local semantics which are difficult to resolve and must be accepted as quirks of NFS. Some of the problems may be avoided (or at least alleviated) by additional intelligence in the client. These are in all cases a result of the stateless nature of the NFS protocol and the fact that the NFS server cannot and should not determine which files the clients have opened.

The most famous example of this behaviour is the deletion of an open file. Applied in the local file system, this leads to the file physically remaining for as long as it is kept open by a process. These semantics cannot be expected in the stateless NFS server. A partial simulation of the local semantics is obtained in that the client renames the file to be deleted in the server; thus, the original file name disappears and the file itself is finally removed on closure. Renamed files have names in the format .*nfsxxxxxxxx*, where *xxxxxxxx* is a number chosen by the client. The files are not usually visible since they begin with a full stop. If the client crashes before the file is closed and before it can remove it, the file is preserved. Thus, on systems which are used as servers, a procedure should be regularly run (for example, on system start-up) to remove these remnant files. This emulation only functions when the opening and deleting processes are on the same client, otherwise the file in question is actually deleted.

This brings us to another problem: under certain circumstances a file may be deleted by another station between two accesses by a client. The server recognizes such situations and rejects further accesses with error code NFSERR_STALE; the user program receives the error code ESTALE. Invalid file handles may be recognized using an additional data field in the file handle and in the inode: in addition to the reference to a file system in the server and to the inode number of the required file therein, the system also stores the generation number of the inode. This generation number is increased by the system when the inode is released (the file is deleted) and on each access the server compares the generation number in the file handle with that in the inode.

Other restrictions are:

- The removal or absence of read or write authorization (with *chmod*) on an open file leads to an error in the case of access other than by the owner of the file (who over NFS always has read and write access to this file in the server). Since program files may also be accessed over NFS, the system reads instructions over NFS using *paging*. For this, the program file must be readable or else it must be executed by the owner himself, otherwise access is rejected by the NFS server. Note in addition that this refers to all files which are already open, where the access authorization is altered during the course of access. As in local file systems, the NFS client verifies the access rights before allowing a file to be opened or a program to be executed. The operation is rejected by the client if there is no authorization, although the server permits it in accordance with the above rules.

- Although the System V file append mode is supported by NFS, appending is not guaranteed when several processes on different clients write simultaneously to a file. This is due to the nature of the implementation, whereby the end of file stored in the file attributes is used as write position. The attributes stored in the client in a cache are usually only updated every three seconds; thus, in the case of multiple access to a file by several clients, they may not necessarily be up to date. In this case, it would be sensible for a programmer to lock the file for the duration of the append operation to prevent overwriting. In the next version of the NFS protocol, problems due to cache inconsistency could be removed, in that a time stamp could be sent to the server to mark the time of the most recent alteration known to the client. If the time stamp were older than the current modification time of the file, the client would receive an error message and could take appropriate measures.

- Write operations whose length exceeds the maximum RPC output length set in the client are not atomic and cannot be mixed with other simultaneous write operations on the same file.

- As for files, directory attributes are also buffered in the client. Since they are only updated every 30 seconds, alterations to the directory may, in certain circumstances, only be visible to another client after this time interval.

- Problems may arise with some UNIX programs in the case of

unsynchronized clocks on the client and server computers, since the time on the server is used for file time stamps. (More about this in the section on the time daemon.)

Simultaneous access of several clients to one server and to the same file may result in data inconsistencies. This is also the case for local file operation; however, here the time windows for inconsistencies are smaller. The current version of NFS avoids additional integrity-related costs to the benefit of the performance in the normal mode of operation and leaves it to the application programs to guard themselves against data inconsistencies by appropriate means, such as file locking.

## NFS and security aspects

Although this chapter and the previous one might give the contrary impression, a UNIX system with NFS is in practice no less secure than a UNIX system without NFS. Basically, we must realize that every time a system is connected to a network the possibility of unauthorized penetration of the system is increased many times over. In NFS implementations to date, sufficient precautions have been taken to make accidental compromise of data difficult. Probably only very few systems could withstand a determined attack, since there are increasingly many loopholes in the day-to-day operation. Version 4.0 of NFS improves security further in that access authorizations are exchanged between client and server in encoded form.

One major security loophole in UNIX is the almost unrestricted privilege of the super-user (user ID 0). All files, without restriction, may be accessed under the login name *root*. Such behaviour is undesirable in networked operation, on security grounds; thus, the user ID 0 in the server is changed to the user ID $-2$. Consequently, files stored in the server under the user *root* have user ID $-2$ as owner. In this way, user ID $-2$ is subjected to the same access restrictions as a normal user. In some systems, user ID $-2$ is entered in */etc/passwd* as *nobody*. Since in the System V data structures the user ID is stored as an unsigned value, $-2$ is 65534 (which can sometimes be confusing).

Version 4.0 of SunOS allows a general conversion of user ID 0 to any other user ID.

This conversion is bypassed by the system call *exportfs*, which can be used to make file systems on most NFS server implementations accessible to the super-user. This is a necessity for diskless workstations which must be able to execute their own system administration with their own files on a server. *exportfs* associates a normal user ID for the super-user access with the file system; all accesses to user ID 0 are then mapped to the ID set apart for this file system. Thus, programs started under the name *root* may access the server, the ID used being individually selectable. The network administrator allocates an individual partition to each diskless workstation with a corresponding 'pseudo super-user ID'.

To prevent unauthorized access to data via RPC requests with falsified user IDs, the NFS server offers the possibility of permitting only RPC requests from privileged port numbers (less than 1024). In this case, higher port numbers are rejected with messages such as `NFS request from unprivileged port, source IP address = 192.9.150.240`. Regrettably, some NFS client implementations use unprivileged port numbers as standard, so that when monitoring is switched on, even mounting by the client is deemed to be unauthorized access. Monitoring may be turned on or off by the network administrator, by setting the variable *nfs_portmon* in the operating system kernel to 1 or 0 (for example, using a debugger). A similar mechanism exists in the mount daemon, in which case however external access by the debugger is usually impossible since it is supplied without a symbol table. Furthermore, the mount daemon may be permitted to compare the Internet address and the name of the client with the local information in */etc/hosts* and to reject requests when there is a discrepancy. All three monitors are normally switched off, although there are systems with other settings.

## The performance of NFS

Since the user under NFS sees no difference between mounted file systems and a local hard disk, he expects the same performance in both cases, which is sometimes impossible. The first limitation is given by the server's hard disk, since, of course, NFS cannot transport the data faster than it can be supplied by this peripheral device. The access speed is also affected by factors such as the performance of the TCP/IP implementation and the Ethernet controller used, which must have sufficient buffer capacity to accept read and write requests of maximum length (8800 bytes).

One should always realize that when NFS is used, system and hard disk are linked not by a highly integrated hard-disk controller specifically designed for this purpose, but by a coaxial cable, two Ethernet controllers and thousands of computer instructions. Satisfactory results can only be expected when these components are optimized to the same extent.

## Mounting NFS file systems

### Method of working

In order to mount a file system on the server, in addition to the NFS server process, the *mount daemon* which executes the MOUNT protocol must also be active. Figure 10.2 gives a schematic representation of the individual

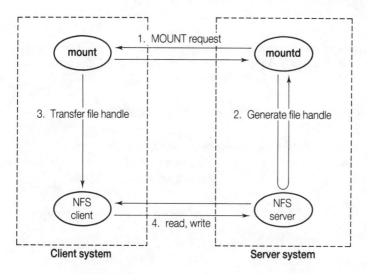

**Figure 10.2**   Execution of a mount procedure.

steps in the execution of a mount procedure.

The program *mountd*, together with *nfsd*, is started when the system is brought up. In the mount procedure, the *mount* command on the client computer makes contact with the mount daemon in order to obtain the first file handle for the root directory of the file system to be mounted. The mount daemon hands the path name of the desired file system, found by the client using the system call *getfh()*, over to the operating system. The latter generates and returns a file handle which is forwarded by the mount daemon to the *mount* command. This file handle is handed over to the NFS client in the operating system together with other entries, including the address of the server computer and other operational parameters, by the system call *mount()*. The NFS client can now generate NFS protocol requests to the server.

## The commands mount and umount

As previously mentioned, NFS file systems are also mounted with the *mount* command. Normally, the *mount* command may be summarized as follows:

```
/etc/mount [−r] specialfile directory
```

In UNIX versions with VFS or FSS, the *mount* command is modified to include entries for the type of the file system in question, so that other objects may be specified in place of special files. When NFS is used, a computer and path name must be given at this point. The new synopsis, initially for System V Version 3, in which the type of the file system to be mounted is given with the −*f* option, is:

> /etc/mount −f NFS[,*options*] *hostname:pathname directory*

BSD versions automatically recognize that a construct of the form 'hostname:pathname' has been given in place of a special file and assume the file system type NFS. Thus, the −*t* option is optional:

> /etc/mount [−t nfs] −o *options hostname:pathname*
>                                              *directory*

In addition to the server and path name entries, options entries are available in both versions which affect the way in which the client operates with this particular file system. Table 10.1 shows the options which exist on both system variants.

On BSD systems, the option *retry* may be used to determine the number of attempts to be made to communicate with the *mountd* computer before abortion. There is also a −*bg* option, whereby, after a first unsuccessful attempt, the command automatically moves to the background and executes subsequent attempts from there. This option is important at system start-up, when the subsequent running of the system should not hang in wait for the mounting of inactive server file systems. The default setting of the *mount* command is such that only one attempt is made, but with a retransmission time of 20 seconds. In addition to *retry* and −*bg*, there are a number of other system-specific options.

In both types of system, the command:

> /etc/umount *directory*

may be used to unmount a file system. Here too BSD systems have additional options for selective unmounting of file systems on specific servers, and so on. The −*a* option is most important: it permits the *umount* command, via broadcast to all mount daemons, to delete all entries for the given client. This function is usually executed as a precaution on system start-up, to remove any entries remaining after a system failure.

Figure 10.3 shows the execution of a mount and unmount procedure as would be executed manually on System V. The network administrator may use the command *showmount* (which we shall go into later) to determine which file systems on the server are accessible.

**Table 10.1**   Options for the *mount* command.

| Option | Effect |
|---|---|
| *soft* | Aborts the operation currently active when the server does not answer after the repetition counter has run out. The program involved receives an error message. Usually, the RPC request is repeated until the server replies (a so-called *hard* mount). |
| *rsize = n* | Sets the maximum transfer size for read operations to $n$ bytes. This prevents the client from requesting too large packets from the server, which, for example, cannot be processed in the UDP implementation or by the Ethernet controller. |
| *wsize = n* | Sets the maximum transfer size for write operations to $n$ bytes. Both transfer sizes should be integers divisible by 1024 and smaller than 8 kbytes. |
| *timeO = n* | Sets the timer for the retransmission of RPC requests in units of 1/10 second. Slow servers may be unnecessarily loaded by a hurried (redundant) retransmission of a request (default is 7/10 second) from the client. When abnormally high retransmission rates occur (see *nfsstat*), checks should be made to see if increasing the waiting time by this option produces an improvement. |
| *retrans = n* | Sets the number of retransmissions of an RPC request in *soft mount* until the operation is terminated. |
| *port = n* | Entry of the port number of the NFS server, if this is not 2049. NFS servers running in parallel with the normal NFS servers on a system (for example, the automounter, which we shall discuss later), must use a different UDP port number. |

## Automatic operation on system start-up and shutdown

There are large differences between System V and BSD systems, particularly in respect of the way in which the system is started up and shut down. For automatic mounting on system start-up of all file systems subsequently required, entries must be made in various files. This is mainly done by hand, although on some systems it is a menu-driven process. We shall only look at this property briefly, without going too far into the system-specific details. In this regard, we note yet again that the greatest differences between UNIX versions from different manufacturers lie in the system management area – thus, the functions described here may be implemented differently, or not at all, on some systems.

In both system variants, the names of the files to be mounted on system start-up are entered in the file */etc/fstab*, although the syntax

```
$ hostname
train2
$ /etc/showmount -e train1
export list for train1:
/usr            train2
$ /etc/mount -f NFS train1:/usr /train1
$ /etc/mount
/ on /dev/dsk/0s1 read/write on Fri Mar 17 09:49:02
/usr on /dev/dsk/0s3 read/write on Fri Mar 17 09:49:35
/usr2 on /dev/dsk/0s4 read/write on Fri Mar 17 09:49:36
/usr1 on /dev/dsk/0s5 read/write on Fri Mar 17 09:49:37
/train1 on train1:/usr read/write on Fri Mar 17 10:51:37
$ /etc/showmount -a train1
train2:/usr
$ /etc/umount /train1
```

**Figure 10.3**   Mount dialogue under System V Release 3.

used is not quite identical in the two cases. In a BSD system, the file system mounted in Figure 10.3 would be declared as:

```
train1:/usr /train1 nfs rw,nosuid 0 0
```

The *nfs* entry specifies the file system type; *rw* says that the system should be readable and writable. This may be followed by several *mount* command options separated by commas. The last two values refer to the file system management: they should both be always 0 for NFS.

In our System V, the entry has the following syntax:

```
train1:/usr /train1 NFS,soft
```

Clearly, the file system type may again be followed by *mount* command options. Entries in */etc/fstab* are recommended since they make the required file systems available automatically on system start-up. As a prerequisite, the server computers chosen should be active. Here, the −*bg* option on BSD systems is helpful, since system start-up is not delayed by repetitions and the servers are automatically mounted after activation. Without this option, if the process breaks down within the predetermined time interval, the mounting must be carried out manually.

File systems may only be unmounted if none of the files they contain has been opened by a process. The same also holds for NFS. If the server is not active at the time of unmounting and thus the mount daemon is unobtainable, delays may arise. On BSD systems, a *umount* with the $-a$ option is usually executed after stopping all user processes.

On System V, the program *fuser* is used to determine whether a file system contains open files. Before file systems are unmounted, programs with open files must be forcibly killed (with the $-K$ option).

## Mount point

When a file system is mounted on a specific directory, that directory becomes a *mount point*. The directory which is used by a client as a mount point may lie anywhere in the server's local file tree, and may itself be in a file system mounted over NFS.

In the server file system, mounted subfile systems are invisible to the client and must be explicitly mounted on the client computer. This restriction prevents the creation of endless mount loops or inefficient mount chains.

## Mount daemon

The mount daemon *mountd* presents itself to the port mapper, like any other RPC service and waits for incoming requests. It has other functions in addition to the issuing of file handles. On the one hand, it has access to the so-called export list, and on the other, it stores the host and path names of all mount processes. In what follows, we shall consider these additional functions of the mount daemon in more detail.

### Export of file systems

The file */etc/exports* is very important for network management, since it contains specifications of whether and by whom a file system may be mounted over NFS. The syntax of the entries is as follows:

pathname [*systemname*|*networkgroup*] ...

Every given file system path name is associated with a list of the client computers or network groups (see later) authorized to mount that file system. If no entry follows a path name, the file system is accessible to all computers. When a path name is specified in */etc/exports*, it should be noted that the mount daemon can only export whole directories; thus, the path name given must represent the first (root) directory of a file system. The mount daemon checks this using the inode number. This restriction has been removed for the first time in SunOS Version 4.0 and System V Release 4.

Within the exported file system, any other directory may be selected

```
all development office training
development (mitsouko,,eng) (aramis,,eng) (balahe,,eng)
office (joop,bogi,off)
training (train1,trainer,train) (train2,trainer,train)
```

**Figure 10.4**   Example of the file */etc/netgroup*.

as the beginning of a subtree. For example, */usr* is usually an individual physical file system containing the directory */usr/bin*. Entry of */usr/bin* in */etc/exports* would have no effect since */usr* must be first exported as a whole, after which the client may mount */usr/bin*. The reason for this lies in the implementation. Without knowing the root of a file system, the server cannot determine whether a file accessed using a file handle is above or below the exported point; this check is needed in order to reject illegal access to unexported parts of a file system.

Computer names are defined in the file */etc/hosts*. Network groups are newly created specially for NFS management and are specified in the file */etc/netgroup*. A *network group* consists of a group name and a list associating computer, user and domain names. Every list element is composed of the following three parts, where an empty field stands for 'undefined':

$$([systemname], [username], [domainname])$$

Network group elements are used for unambiguous definition of objects, for example, user $x$ on computer $y$ in domain $z$. The definition of domains and their functions is described in detail in the section on YP.

The entry of the user name is required for the definition of user groups but is initially unimportant to the mount process. We discuss the use of network groups in the */etc/passwd* file in more detail in the section on YP.

As shown in Figure 10.4, the definition of a network group may also contain references to other network groups. This provides for the generation of recursive structures which are easier to manage.

In the file */etc/exports*, it is very easy to determine groups of computers from the same domain. Figure 10.5 shows the listing of the network group defined above. Here, the file system */usr1* is only reserved for selected computers, while the other file systems are accessible by several groups. Naturally, computer and network group names may also be mixed, as can be seen in the second line.

```
/usr all
/usr/src development train2
/usr1 anteus fidji dior
```

**Figure 10.5**   Example of the file */etc/exports*.

## Commands for the network administrator

Figure 10.3 shows an application of the command */etc/showmount* which communicates with the mount daemon. We may use the −*e* option of this command to interrogate the contents of a */etc/exports* file. Other options are −*a* for a list of all mount entries and −*d* for a list of all active mounted file systems. The mount daemon stores this information in the file */etc/rmtab* and thus preserves it between two system starts. *showmount* usually talks to the local mount daemon, but it also understands the entry of a computer name and in this case directs the enquiry to the appropriate mount daemon. Thus, it is possible to find out about the lists on other servers.

The computer names provided by *showmount* may, for example, be used by *rwall*. The network administrator uses this command to send a message to the terminals of all users of a given host, as in the local *wall* command. The options of *rwall* allow the entry of host names and network groups. If, for example, it is decided to take down an NFS server, all client computers should be informed, as shown in Figure 10.6.

*showmount* uses the MOUNT protocol for its mount daemon enquiries. *rwall* and the corresponding *rwalld* process use their own RPC-based protocol.

```
$ rwall 'showmount'
Server train2 has to be rebooted,
please logoff immediately.
$
```

**Figure 10.6**   Use of *rwall*.

```
$ rpcinfo -p
program vers proto port
100004    2    udp  1027  ypserv
100004    2    tcp  1025  ypserv
100004    1    udp  1027  ypserv
100004    1    tcp  1025  ypserv
100017    1    tcp  1032  rexd
100012    1    udp  1082  sprayd
100008    1    udp  1084  walld
100005    1    udp  1086  mountd
100002    1    udp  1088  rusersd
100002    2    udp  1088  rusersd
100001    1    udp  1091  rstatd
100001    2    udp  1091  rstatd
100001    3    udp  1091  rstatd
100003    2    udp  2049  nfs
$
```

**Figure 10.7**  Output from *rpcinfo*.

## Diagnosis of RPC and NFS problems

### rpcinfo

The port mapper (implemented by the program *portmap*) is one of the most important members of the chain of stations which a request must pass through between the client and the server; connections to the server are impossible without it. The program *rpcinfo* deals not only with the local port mapper, but also directly with the port mappers of other computers. It may be used to display the contents of the port/program number tables and is even able to activate individual servers for test purposes. Thus, it can provide considerable help in the diagnosis of RPC problems. The call:

        rpcinfo -p [*hostname*]

provides the user with a list of the RPC programs registered with the port mapper (see Figure 10.7). If a requested RPC service is not listed here, the corresponding server must be restarted. This may be the case when the port mapper is only started up after this server or when the original registration of the server has been lost due to a crash of the port mapper. If the port mapper cannot be contacted, an error message is given, which in certain cases provides further information about the source of the error. Error messages such as `rpcinfo: can't contact port mapper: RPC: Remote system error - 125` are usually indications of a fundamental problem. In this case, it should be checked whether any contact at all with the server computer is possible, for example, using the program *ping*.

    *rpcinfo* may also be used to access specific individual RPC programs. The call:

    `rpcinfo -u localhost mountd`

checks the functional integrity of the local mount dæmon. Depending on whether the RPC program in question is offered over UDP or TCP, the $-u$ or $-t$ option must be used. To test the server, *rpcinfo* sends a request to procedure 0 of the corresponding program and waits for an answer. If everything is in order, the following message appears, as for the previous example:

    `program 100005 version 1 ready and waiting`

Otherwise an error message is given with a reference. An *rpcinfo* test call may be summarized as follows:

    `/etc/rpcinfo -[u|t]` *systemname program* `[`*versionnumber*`]`

The RPC program may be specified as both a program number and (as in our example) a program name. The mapping of symbolic program names to program numbers is made in the file */etc/rpc*. This information is shown on the port mapper listing after the port number. We note moreover that some RPC programs, such as NFS, already use a version of their protocol higher than version 1 and in this case the number of the desired version must be given after the program name.

    In the most recent version of *rpcinfo* in SunOS 4.0, all RPC servers of a program may be simultaneously tested by broadcast, using the $-b$ option. Of course, a broadcast only functions for UDP-based services.

    One more piece of advice: there may be many reasons why an RPC program cannot be reached. Debugging should be carried out gradually step by step, checking all RPC stations on a message route one after the other, possibly using commands from the TCP/IP area such as *ping*, *netstat*, etc.

## nfsstat

In debugging, statistics about the number and type of RPC requests to the NFS server, the calls of the NFS client and other NFS-related processes in the operating system kernel may be extremely helpful. The command *nfsstat* exists for this purpose and calling it produces the output shown in Figure 10.8 as standard. Normally, both client and server statistics are shown, but the options $-c$ and $-s$ limit the output to client or server statistics. The $-z$ option sets all internal system statistical counters to 0 and may only be used by the network administrator. The options $-r$ and $-n$ are used to show only the RPC or the NFS statistics.

RPC statistics provide very important information for diagnosis of problems. They provide information about possible problems at the transport level. The counter *badcalls* contains the total number of all defective RPC messages; *nullrecv* and *badlen* refer to empty or short RPC messages; *xdrcall* stands for errors in decoding call parameters. The counter *wait* is increased when no UDP communication end points are free to send, and *badxid* counts the number of received messages which were not answers to immediately preceding RPC requests. The *timeout* and *retrans* entries in the client are of particular importance. If errors are indicated here, one of the NFS servers connected to the client is either too slow or it is losing UDP packets. In this case, it is advisable (see *mount* command) to increase the RPC request retransmission waiting time for this server or, in certain circumstances, to decrease the size of read or write operations, to avoid overflow of one's own, or the server's, receive buffer. (There are no problems in experimenting here until the optimal setting is found – there is no need to be afraid of damage.)

# Lock manager

## Background

System V and some other UNIX derivatives offer the facility to lock file regions for a period of time against read or write accesses. Such locking prevents several programs from making simultaneous alterations or read accesses while the data is inconsistent due to modifications. The available *file* and *record locking* operations are among other things implemented in the System V call *fcntl*.

Since NFS was developed on a BSD-based system where record locking was not defined, file locking was impossible in the earliest versions of NFS (up to 3.2). This function was first introduced when the demand for compatible interfaces for NFS and a complete mapping of the local file system semantics became vociferous. Naturally, file locking in a network is a good deal more complicated than in a local file system and the consequences are correspondingly more far reaching.

```
$ nfsstat
Server rpc:
calls        badcalls nullrecv badlen   xdrcall
8637         0        0        0        0

Server nfs:
calls        badcalls
8632         0
null         getattr  setattr  root     lookup
1  0%        25 0%    1  0%    0  0%    8177 94%
readlink     read     wrcache  write    create
0  0%        4  0%    0  0%    1  0%    2  0%
remove       rename   link     symlink  mkdir
1  0%        0  0%    1  0%    0  0%    1  0%
rmdir        readdir  fsstat
1  0%        413 4%   4  0%

Client rpc:
calls        badcalls retrans  badxid   timeout
8631         1        0        0        0
wait         newcred
0            0

Client nfs:
calls        badcalls nclget   nclsleep
8631         0        8631     0
null         getattr  setattr  root     lookup
0  0%        25 0%    1  0%    0  0%    8177 94%
readlink     read     wrcache  write    create
0  0%        4  0%    0  0%    1  0%    2  0%
remove       rename   link     symlink  mkdir
1  0%        0  0%    1  0%    0  0%    1  0%
rmdir        readdir  fsstat
1  0%        413 4%   4  0%
$
```

Figure 10.8   Output from *nfsstat*.

## Realization

The most important point is that file locking is handled not by the NFS protocol but as an additional RPC service parallel to it. This corresponds to one of the RPC philosophies that requires a 'particular protocol for a particular task'. Secondly, as already mentioned, NFS is a stateless protocol and there is no way that a function such as file locking may be resident there.

The NFS *locking service* is one of the most complicated services within NFS; it consists of several protocols and server programs. The philosophy behind Sun's implementation in SunOS makes the matter rather more complicated, since the tables to store locks are not implemented in the operating system but in an individual process, the lock daemon, *lockd*. This means that the SunOS operating system must communicate with the lock daemon, even for local locks. For this, it uses an RPC protocol over UDP called the *Kernel Lock Manager* (KLM) protocol. Every lock operation is firstly notified to the *lockd* process, which then decides whether the lock operation should be sent to a further *lockd* or whether it is a matter of a local operation.

The RPC protocol for communication between remote lock daemons goes under the name of the *Network Lock Manager* (NLM) protocol. Lock daemons may be both NLM clients and servers. There are various versions of NLM: when a computer is to be used as NFS server for PC-NFS and MS-DOS 3.1, compatible locking is required – at least Version 3 is needed.

The form of implementation chosen by Sun, at least for local lock operations as against kernel-based implementations as in System V, implies a clear loss of performance. In NFS implementations for System V, there is also the problem of consistency between the internal and external system lock tables in the lock daemon. Thus, some manufacturers have introduced modifications to the implementation of the locking service or have developed their own RPC protocols for communication between lock daemons and the operating system kernel. Not for these reasons alone the locking service has become a problem child for some manufacturers, with the consequence that it is not even supplied in some cases. A service which is not generally available will scarcely be used by software developers as a basis for applications – therefore, the need for its existence again decreases.

## Status monitor

One of the most important points in the lock operation is the question of how long the participating computers are active. We shall consider an example for clarity. Let us assume that a process on computer A has locked a region in a file in a file system mounted over NFS on computer B. If B now receives a request for the same region from computer C, there are two possibilities: either B waits (under certain circumstances for ever) until the end of A's process, or it checks whether A is hanging in the network (crashed). If this is the case, the locking process no longer exists and the region is immediately released to C (via B). The so-called *status monitor* *statd* exists to monitor the activity of computers.

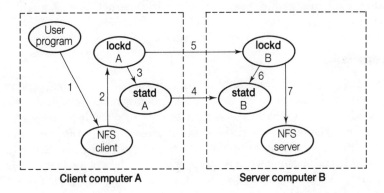

**Figure 10.9**    Execution of a lock procedure.

Figure 10.9 shows the execution of a lock operation in the network. Let us examine the function of the status monitor with an example:

(1)   A user program on computer A generates a request to the system to lock a region of a file.

(2)   The lock daemon on computer A receives a request from the NFS client module in the system to lock a file in computer B.

(3)   A's lock daemon registers itself with A's local status monitor via an RPC procedure. The RPC request contains as parameters a call-back procedure in the lock daemon and the host name of the computer to be monitored (B).

(4)   A's status monitor turns to B's status monitor which stores the host name of the requesting computer A as a file name in the directory /etc/sm.

(5)   After the monitoring has started, using an RPC request, the lock daemon A transfers the desired lock to the lock daemon on computer B.

(6)   Lock daemon B permits the monitoring of computer A.

(7)   Finally, it locks the file.

If computer B with status monitor and lock daemon crashes, after a subsequent restart, status monitor B processes the stored list of host names and informs status monitor A of the restart. The latter informs lock daemon A who reclaims the previous lock in lock daemon B.

As this example shows, the monitoring does not involve the regular exchange of messages but feedback when the crashed status monitor is restarted.

## System failure

As in other NFS services, so too for network-wide locking, the first commandment is transparency to local file system semantics. When a server crashes, after restart, the lock service attempts to reproduce the status as it was before the crash, so that the application running on the client should notice nothing of the interruption other than a time delay. Of course, this is only possible and sensible when a server crashes; failure of a client computer would also destroy the context of the application. In this case, the server can and must release the lock of a process which has ceased to exist. In both cases, the partner involved knows nothing of the interruption until the computer which crashed is restarted, and under certain circumstances this may lead to long delays.

After system start-up, before the lock manager passes over to normal operation, it waits for a short time called the *grace period*. During this time interval, client computers have the possibility of reinstalling locks in place before a possible crash. New locks may only be requested after this waiting period. As a standard, the grace period is 45 seconds, but it may be changed on activation of *lockd*.

If it is impossible for the client to reinstall a lock after a server is restarted, the client's lock daemon sends the process in question a newly defined signal for the lock service, SIGLOST. The SIGLOST signal behaves like other UNIX signals: the process may either take notice of it and institute recovery measures or ignore it (normally, the process is then itself terminated). This process may seem somewhat infuriating, but the alternative would be to work with possibly corrupted data.

## Restrictions

Set against the locking implemented in System V, locking over the NFS lock service has only a few restrictions:

(1) The lock daemon does not seek to identify *deadlocks*; thus, two programs may potentially lock each other out. In System V and XENIX, local deadlocks are recognized, but a network-wide protection of this type would be associated with disproportionate expense.

(2) The reference implementation on BSD-based systems supports only *advisory* locking: only co-operating programs, which check whether locks are present before the access, experience the existence of any locking. Mandatory locking is not a function of the lock service but

must be implemented in the operating system in the NFS file system code of the client computer. In this case, the operating system ensures that a locked file region cannot be accidentally accessed.

# Network Information Service

## Overview

As discussed in the previous chapter, the NIS service, previously called the YP service, is used to distribute information in the network. Usually, for reasons of operational security, several YP servers are active: a master and several so-called slave servers.

The YP information consists primarily of pertinent files in the directory */etc*. While central storage in the case of */etc/passwd* and */etc/group* is an implicit prerequisite for the operational security of NFS, YP is only used to simplify the administration for other maps already defined on installation. However, the YP service is not restricted to these files; the network administrator may extend it to include arbitrary maps.

As soon as YP services are active, only the maps for */etc/hosts*, */etc/networks*, */etc/ethers*, */etc/services*, */etc/protocols* and */etc/rpc* are accessed. If the YP server is started up with the $-i$ option, it independently turns to a BIND server if search operations in the *hosts* map are unsuccessful. As always, the files themselves must nevertheless exist and contain at least all the information required at system start-up (at the instant before YP becomes active). In particular, the entries in */etc/hosts* with the addresses of one's own network interfaces must be present at system start-up.

The definition of network groups is read only from YP. Network groups may be accessed via the files */etc/passwd*, */etc/group*, */etc/exports*, */etc/hosts/.equiv* and *$HOME/.rhosts*.

Currently, there are two versions of the YP protocol (Versions 1 and 2) which, for upward compatibility, are simultaneously supported from NFS 3.0. The YP service is available under TCP and UDP.

## Administrative domains

The concept of *domains* is introduced to simplify the management of an NFS network. Thus, a domain consists of a group of computers which belong together for technical administrative purposes (for example, belonging to the same department, the same network section or the like).

There is no functional relationship between an NFS domain and an Internet domain, although the same intention underlies both. In practice, the network administrator will seek to maintain a congruence between both domains, since to some extent similar information, such as Internet addresses, must be managed in both systems.

The *domain name* may be up to 255 characters long and is entered into the computer via the command *domainname*, usually at system start-up. Entry of a domain name is essential to the functioning of the YP subsystem, since maps are only valid within a domain. Thus, the YP client must be able to determine which domain it is in, in order to access the YP server responsible for this domain.

## Configuration

### Master and slave servers

After installation of NFS and YP on the computer, the YP subsystem must be configured. There is usually an array of utilities for this, which facilitate the work. On some systems, a menu-driven shell is also available.

Before the YP subsystem is configured (if this has not already been done), a domain name must be chosen and a computer selected as master server. Every map within the domain is assigned to a master server. Usually, all maps of a domain have the same master server, although this is not mandatory. The network administrator could set up maps on a specific server (computer). As soon as such special configurations are required, the network administrator must be able to cope without the utilities which are otherwise present.

The remaining computers are configured with slave servers. One YP server per domain is theoretically sufficient, but, for reasons of robustness, several servers are usual. Otherwise, it may happen that, after the failure of the master server, it is impossible to login to the system, since even the login process accesses information in the *passwd* map. When servers are running on several computers, it is very unlikely that not a single server is active. If a YP server is configured on every computer in the network, we know that the local YP server at least is always active. In NFS networks with diskless workstations, the argument at this point is somewhat different: these local workstations do not need a local YP server since NFS and YP servers usually run on the same server computer, and if the server computer crashes, operation is in principle no longer possible. Basically, the following rule holds: the more YP servers there are, the greater the protection against failure. In addition, practice teaches us that computers are less likely to crash than to be shut down or reconfigured.

Depending on the system, the files and network management commands belonging to the YP subsystem are found in the files */usr/etc/yp* or */etc/yp*. From SunOS 4.0 or System V.4, the files will be held in */var*. The installation of the YP subsystem uses the Shell script *ypinit*. *ypinit* has two options: −*m* to install a master server and −*s* to install a slave server. It automatically sets up the required directories and it transforms the local files in /etc into maps in the case of a master server or fetches the maps from the master in the case of a slave server. The computer names of the slave servers are stored in a separate map called *ypservers*. Figure 10.10 shows the installation of a master server.

### ypserv

The YP server program *ypserv* implements the YP protocol and is an RPC service which, like all other services, registers itself with the port mapper.

A map consists of several data records with a key to search for individual entries. In addition to the data records, each map has two extra internal entries: the key YP_LAST_MODIFIED may be used to request the generation number and YP_MASTER_NAME requests the name of the master server.

*ypserv* searches for maps in the YP directory and in subdirectories with domain names, for example, */usr/etc/yp/domainname*. This means that the YP server must be able to serve several domains simultaneously. Since maps in the subdirectories are automatically served by the server, the network administrator can easily install his own maps.

### makedbm

Maps must be held in a special database format generated by the command *makedbm*. The corresponding dbm routines were originally available as *libdbm.a* in UNIX Version 7 but have not been retained in System V. On BSD systems whose genesis also goes back to Version 7, this library still exists. The routines contained in it implement a mini-database with a single variable-length key. *makedbm* is a utility to generate such a database map, which basically consists of two files. One file ending in *.pag* holds the data records; the second data file, which ends in *.dir*, holds the hash codes and access references.

A *makedbm* data input record consists of a line with a key and the associated data, where all characters up to a tab or a space character are interpreted as a key. The special entries for generation number and master server are generated automatically by *makedbm*, although they may be modified at will with command line options. The input files such as */etc/passwd* may be brought to the *makedbm* input format using *awk* scripts. The YP directory contains a *makefile* which provides all the information needed to generate the standard maps. It is also used by *ypinit* and when altering maps (see 'Administration' section to follow).

Existing maps may be displayed using the −*u* option (see Figure 10.11).

Since the dbm routines only support one key per data record, it is usual to generate several maps with different *indices* from the data

```
# ypinit -m
```
Installing the yp database will require that you answer a
few questions.  Questions will all be asked at the beginning
of the procedure.

Do you want this procedure to quit
on non-fatal errors?  [y/n:  n] y

At this point, we have to construct a list of the hosts
which will run yp servers.  train1 is in the list of yp
server hosts.  Please continue to add the names for the
other hosts, one per line.
When you are done with the list, type a <ctl D>.
next host to add: *train1*
next host to add: *train2*
next host to add: ^D

The current list of yp servers looks like this:
train1
train2


Is this correct?  [y/n:  y] y
There will be no further questions.  The remainder of the
procedure should take 5 to 10 minutes.

Building /etc/yp/ixtrain/ypservers...
/etc/yp/makedbm /tmp/yp3390 /etc/yp/ixtrain/ypservers
Running /etc/yp /Makefile...
updated passwd
updated group
updated services
updated protocols


train1 has been set up as a yp master server without any
errors.  If there are running slave yp servers, run yppush
now for any databases which have been changed.  If there are
no running slaves, run ypinit on those hosts which are
to be slave servers.
```

**Figure 10.10**   Output from *ypinit*.
```

```
$ /usr/etc/yp/makedbm −u /usr/etc/yp/ixos/group.bygid
YP_LAST_MODIFIED 0625443567
YP_MASTER_NAME aramis
100 ixos::100:
12 daemon::12:root,daemon
6 mail::6:root
5 uucp::5:uucp
4 adm::4:root,adm,daemon
3 sys::3:root,bin,sys,adm
2 bin::2:root,bin,daemon
1 other::1:
0 root::0:root
$
```

**Figure 10.11**    Output of a YP map with *makedbm −u*.

in the same file. For example, for */etc/group*, in addition to a map *group.byname* in which the group names act as keys, a map called *group.bygid* is generated which contains the group IDs as keys. Figure 10.11 shows the last version. The YP client should use one or other of these maps, depending on whether it is searching for the group name or for a group ID. The same is true of */etc/passwd* and most other maps.

The *makefile* for the YP configuration automatically generates various indices; the existence of different indices is usually hidden to the YP user. However, some management commands require the explicit entry of the correct version of a map; thus, one should be familiar with the concept.

## Access to maps

### Indirect access from programs

Maps replace or supplement a range of files in the system: as soon as YP is in operation, the files cannot and should not be accessed, only the YP server. Consequently, not only a large number of the UNIX commands, but also other programs, which access the above files in some way (and there are more than a few of these), must be modified. These include important commands such as *login*, *ps*, *ls* and all TCP/IP commands. The modifications must be made in such a way that, as before, the commands also function without YP systems and are able to read the appropriate files when necessary in the case of outages of the YP subsystem.

## Program interfaces

Access to the files contained in */etc* is usually via the routines in the C library such as *getpwuid()*, *getgrnam()*, *gethostbyname()*, *getprotoent()*, etc. These routines are modified on NFS systems so that they may have recourse to the YP servers when the YP subsystem is active. All programs which use these routines must therefore only be relinked for operation with YP. Unfortunately, this must be done for all existing programs.

## User interfaces

Two commands are available for use in Shell scripts or for the display of maps on the screen, namely, *ypcat* and *ypmatch*. These output a map in full or in records. Both commands have the following options:

- −*d* Name of another administrative domain.
- −*k* Output of the key value before the data record.
- −*x* Output of the conversion table for map names, which, for example, converts the entry *passwd* into *passwd.byname*. The name alone is known as a *nickname*.
- −*t* Suppression of nickname conversion.

Figure 10.12 shows the use of both commands on the screen. First, the map name conversion table is output, followed by the *group* map (actually *group.byname*). The subsequent call to *ypmatch* searches for the entry for the group *ixos* in the same map and then queries the same record, this time over the group ID index (*group.bygid*).

## Associating files and maps

Since the files */etc/group* and */etc/passwd* are held in YP for all computers in the network, they could actually be deleted from the local file system. But, even in a fail-safe system such as YP, it may happen that not a single server is obtainable. However, since the access to the information in the password file is essential for entry to the system, in such a case no one would be able to login to the system to eliminate the cause of failure. Moreover, the network administrator must also be able to make computer-specific entries, such as the location of the Login directory for a login name or the closure of individual login names. For this reason, both files are retained and their syntax is extended in such a way that they may be combined with the information in the maps.

```
$ ypcat -x
Use "passwd" for map "passwd.byname"
Use "group" for map "group.byname"
Use "networks" for map "networks.byaddr"
Use "hosts" for map "hosts.byaddr"
Use "protocols" for map "protocols.bynumber"
Use "services" for map "services.byname"
Use "aliases" for map "mail.aliases"
Use "ethers" for map "ethers.byname"
$ ypcat group
daemon::12:root,daemon
other::1:
uucp::5:uucp
root::0:root
mail::6:root
ixos::100:
sys::3:root,bin,sys,adm
bin::2:root,bin,daemon
adm::4:root,adm,daemon
$ ypmatch ixos group
ixos::100:
$ ypmatch 100 group.bygid
ixos::100:
$
```

**Figure 10.12**   Screen dialogue with *ypcat* and *ypmatch*.

## Syntax

A YP entry begins with a '+' sign at the beginning of a line. A '@' sign after the '+' means that this refers to a network group.

In */etc/passwd* and */etc/group*, the above may be followed by fields separated by a colon, where an entry in a field means that the value entered locally replaces the value in the map.

In the example in Figure 10.13, the entry *christa* is taken, without alteration, from YP, *santi* is given a new Login directory. The members of the network group *training* can no longer login to the system since their password entries have been invalidated. All other users are allocated the entry Guest in the GECOS field.

The '+@' syntax is used in */etc/hosts.equiv* and *$HOME/.rhosts* as well as in */etc/passwd*. Here, there is also a −@ entry which may be used to define unambiguous network group combinations.

```
root:2zFsHfeqselC.:0:3:0000-Admin(0000):/:
sysadm::0:0:general system administration:/usr/admin:
powerdown:pxHL.g5d.2wSQ:0:0:power down machine:/usr/admin:
+christa:
+santi:::::/usr/santi:
+@training:NOLOGIN:
+:::Guest
```

**Figure 10.13**   Password file with YP extensions.


## Administration

### Modification of maps

In the course of operation, it will from time to time be necessary to supplement, modify or delete entries in the maps. For this, the alterations must be implemented in the master server computer and a *make* activated in the YP directory. This command generates a new file map and distributes it automatically to the slave servers.

It is very important to transfer an altered map to all slave servers most promptly, since the YP servers are freely selectable by the YP clients. Map inconsistencies may lead to reactions which appear inexplicable to the user, and it usually takes some time before the cause is discovered. The names of all slave servers are stored in the map *ypservers*. When a new slave server is installed in the network, it must be included in this map, since otherwise it is not included in the distribution of altered maps. Slave servers which are not active at the time of the distribution will not receive the alteration. Thus, it is advisable to fetch the maps periodically from the master server oneself. The network administrator may instigate regular distribution of the current maps from the master server via *cron* and the Shell scripts */etc/yp/ypxfr1pdy*, */etc/yp/ypxfr1phr* and */etc/yp/ypxfr2pdy*.

The maps are fetched by the program *ypxfr* on the slave server. The program *yppush* is used by the master server to initiate the sending of maps; it sees to it that all slave servers receive altered maps via *ypxfr* and checks that the transfer was successful.


### Map diagnosis

The command *yppoll* supplies the version number of a map together with the domain it supports and the name of the master server. This information is important, for example, if inconsistencies between two servers are found. Note here that the full map name (for example, *passwd.byname*) should be given and not the nickname.

## *ypbind*

In the previous sections, we explained why several YP servers should run in the network. When an application program requires information from a map, it must first find out which YP server it should turn to (it should seek an active YP server). This search would be carried out for all programs which access YP each time a program is activated and would put a load on the network and on the other computers in it. Thus, an extra service has been inserted between the YP client and the YP server, the so-called YP binder. The YP binder carries out a one-off search on behalf of the YP client of a computer to find the Internet address of an active server in the network and then stores this address.

The *ypbind* daemon must be active on every computer on which YP is activated, since the YP client can only address requests for the address of a YP server to the local *ypbind*. If *ypbind* has stored the address of a server, it returns it immediately to the YP client; if it does not have such an address it begins to search for a YP server using the YPBIND RPC protocol.

The port mapper's broadcast function is used for this purpose. Figure 10.14 shows a schematic representation of such a search procedure. For every request from a YP client for a valid YP server address, *ypbind* checks that the YP server at the stored Internet address is in fact still active. (The corresponding computer may have been shut down in the meantime.) If the YP server is no longer active, a search is automatically made for another active YP server and the following message is displayed on the console of the client computer:

```
yp: server not responding for domain yzx; still trying
```

This message is regularly repeated and terminates when a search is finally successful with:

```
yp: server for domain xyz OK
```

Checking the YP server has the knock-on effect of distributing the load in the YP subsystem. If an overloaded YP server does not answer within the expected time interval, the YP binder instigates a change to another YP server. The additional load is transferred to that YP server which is first to reply to the broadcast of the YP binder; that is, is the least loaded and most efficient computer.

*ypbind* can support several domains simultaneously and can store a separate server address for each different domain. For most commands, the current domain is used when there is no entry.

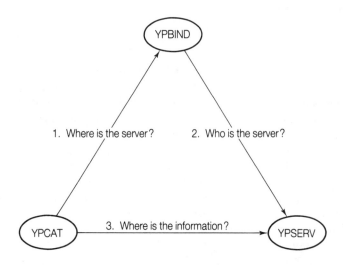

**Figure 10.14**   Execution of the YPBIND process.

Activation of *ypbind* it not initially followed by further actions: the program only waits for requests. *ypbind* only begins the search for a YP server on receiving the very first request; thus, when a command with YP access is first used there may be short delays. Annoyingly, it is only then that one notices whether at least one server is active – when no servers are active one may have some time to wait. Normally, this contact is established on the first attempt to login to the computer, thus creating a very irritating situation. In fact, it is necessary to login to **/etc/passwd** under a local management login name and sort the problem out from there, since the login program is doggedly waiting for the reply from *ypbind* and access remains blocked. In this case, only one thing helps – switching off the computer, starting it up again and immediately entering a local management login name.

## Administrative commands

### *ypwhich*

*ypwhich* communicates directly with *ypbind* and thus permits queries of the Internet address stored momentarily by *ypbind*. It outputs the name of the computer whose *ypserv* is used for requests by the YP client. If a local

```
$ hostname
train2
$ ypwhich
train2
$ ypwhich train2
train1
$ ypset train1
$ ypwhich
train1
$ ypset train2
$ ypwhich
train2
$
```

**Figure 10.15**   Use of *ypwhich* and *ypset*.

YP server is active, one's own computer name will usually appear, since this *ypserv* is the quickest to answer. Otherwise the name of a computer in the network appears here. By giving a computer name as an argument, it is possible to find out which master server is responsible for a given slave server.

Other options permit queries of the YP master server relating to individual maps or entry of other domains. *ypwhich* may be used by all users.

### ypset

The setting stored in *ypbind* may be altered from the outside. The command *ypset*, which is only accessible by the network administrator, is used for this.

If a computer name or an Internet address is given when calling *ypset*, *ypbind* is instructed to use this computer as YP server in the future (see Figure 10.15). However, *ypbind* only checks this address when a client submits a request. In the case of error, another server in the network is then sought.

Other options allow another domain to be given or *ypbind* to be configured on another computer. Note here that if a computer name is given, this name must be converted into the Internet address. However, in certain circumstances this is only possible if the YP server is reachable. Thus, direct entry of the Internet address is the best way in the case of error.

### yppasswd

Changing the password of a login name means a change in the file
*/etc/passwd*. In YP operation, the alteration must be undertaken on
the master server. The *yppasswd* command replaces the UNIX command
*passwd* on NFS systems with YP subsystems: here, every user may change
his password directly in the map. On the master server computer, there
must be an active *yppasswdd* daemon which makes the changes in the
master file and distributes the updated map to the slave servers.

The behaviour of *yppasswd* is almost identical to that of the normal
*passwd* command, although the old and the new passwords are transmitted
in a single RPC message. Since the new password is only accepted when
the old one is correctly entered, errors are first noticed in the *yppasswdd*
server.

## NFS-based services

## REX

In order to execute programs on other computers, the command *rsh* is
usually used. This command creates a new run-time environment on the
other computers. Sometimes one only requires to run a program on another
computer where the data to be processed is stored locally. When *rsh* is used,
this data must (as far as possible) be transferred to the other computer in
a pipe or via *rcp*. In some cases, this restriction makes it impractical to
use *rsh*. Another problem arises because *rsh* does not export the local
environment variables of the calling process to the server computer and so
the run-time environment there is not identical with that locally. Often
tedious additional typing of parameters is necessary.

The installation of NFS brings with it new possibilities for file access:
it is no longer necessary to copy files to other computers; instead, processes
may be permitted direct access. The data remains in the same computer,
and the processing takes place where the necessary resources or a particular
program are located. The support needed for such a mode of operation is
provided by the *Remote Execution Service* (REX).

### on and rexd

The *on* command is the client program of the REX service. It works
alongside the *rexd* daemon as server. The syntax for *on* is as follows:

```
on [-i] [-n] systemname command [parameter]
```

```
$ hostname
aramis
$ cat >fred
That is a text line.
^D
$ rsh mitsouko cat fred
cat:   cannot open fred
$ on mitsouko cat fred
That is a text line.
$
```

**Figure 10.16**    Execution of the *on* command.

*on* sends further information with the command to be executed and its
parameters to the *rexd* computer. This provides for an identical run-time
environment with the following steps:

- Creation of a process with the same user and group IDs.

- Transfer of the environment variables.

- The current directory of the *on* process is mounted in a temporary
  directory on the server using NFS, if it is not already mounted
  elsewhere.

- If it is desired to run an interactive program, such as a screen editor,
  (option $-i$), the current options of the local terminal driver are
  exported. In this case, as in *telnet* and *rlogin*, a pseudo terminal
  is also used.

*on* and *rexd* communicate using RPC requests and use TCP as transport
protocol. Figure 10.16 shows the creation of a local file and the output of
its contents to the screen using a *cat* initiated on the server computer. In
this way, it is possible for application programs which are only present in
specific computers in the network to process data throughout the network,
without the user copying the data and without starting a session on this
computer.

## Automounter

SunOS 4.0 provides another higher-level service which is implemented using
NFS, namely, the *automounter* (Callaghan and Lyon, 1989). This makes it
possible to mount file systems on other computers only when required and

transparently to the user. This prevents the permanent mounting of a large number of (often unrequired) file systems on workstations.

We shall use an example to give a closer insight into the functional description of the automounter. Imagine that on your workstation there is a directory */src* containing several subdirectories for further file trees. In fact, these file trees are not local but are stored on servers in the network. Accessing a file in one of the subdirectories, for example, */src/test/test.c*, leads to the automatic mounting of the file system *test* by NFS and the execution of the operation (for example, reading of *test.c*) as though the file system were always in its place. After some time, when there has been no further access to the data tree, */src/test* is automatically unmounted without further ado.

The automounter makes very clever use of various functions of the UNIX operating system and of NFS. It represents a local NFS server which is treated by the operating system like any other NFS server on a computer. The automounter NFS server manages a virtual file system, which is mounted in a directory */src* using the *mount* command. If a user accesses a file */src/test/test.c* in this directory, the operating system must first search through the path name. Thus, in order to find a directory *test* in */src* an NFS LOOKUP request is sent by the operating system to the automounter NFS server. If the underlying file system is not yet mounted, the automounter creates a mount point in a temporary directory */tmp_mnt* and mounts the actual file system from the remote server there. The trick is that the automounter simulates a symbolic link from the target directory */src/test* to the temporary mount point and returns a file handle for a symbolic link in the result of the *lookup* call. The operating system then follows the symbolic link to the target point */tmp_mnt/test/test.c* using a *readlink* call to the automounter NFS server. If the symbolic link is unused for more than five minutes (standard setting), the automounter attempts to unmount the file system again. This mode of operation of the automounter is known as *indirect mapping*. In *direct mapping*, the automounter NFS server is mounted at various points, from which it provides access to a specific individual file system.

The mapping of automount points to NFS server computers and to file systems on them may be carried out in local files or in YP maps. The network administrator may use YP maps to specify a fixed mapping for whole groups of computers (for example, directories for the on-line manual or a source code hierarchy). This flexible configuration means that the possible uses of the automounter are manifold.

The automounter is one of the few commercially available examples of the species of 'NFS special servers' which are implemented as user programs and not as part of the operating system kernel. Sadly, in general, the facilities offered by the NFS protocol are still too little understood and used. Other uses for special servers include CD ROM disk drives and juke boxes for optical disks and archiving systems.

# NFS specialities

## Time daemon

Some UNIX programs take run-time decisions based on the time entries in a file. For example, the development tool *make* compares the modification times of source texts with those of the programs to be generated from them; if the source file consists of younger data, a new compilation and linking process is restarted. When a new file is generated over NFS access, the current time of the server, and not that of the client, is entered in the file attribute in the file system catalogue (inode). Since the system clocks of the client and the server almost certainly have different settings, this systematic comparison of client and server time entries may lead to unexpected behaviour, unless particular steps are taken to synchronize the two clocks.

This is not the only reason why the *timed* daemon (which is also supplied with NFS) has existed since 4.3BSD. The time daemons on all computers in the network exchange messages among themselves in order to synchronize the system clocks of the computers exactly to within a few milliseconds. To do this, they use the system call *adjtime* which slows or accelerates its own system clock in order to gradually effect the desired time adjustment. Regrettably, *adjtime* is not implemented in most versions of System V and so *timed* loses its meaning. The only countermeasure on these computers is to adjust the system clocks manually as exactly as possible.

## pcnfsd

*pcnfsd* is an RPC server which was specially developed for joint working with PC-NFS, the NFS version for MS-DOS computers. Its tasks are the assignment of access rights and the allocation of a spool service. Some of the details of this program are the following. On MS-DOS computers, user or group IDs, which under NFS must be sent as a component part of every RPC request, are not present. Thus, before mounting an NFS file system on their PC, PC-NFS users must execute a sort of login, during which they supply a login name and a password. These two values are transferred by an RPC client integrated into PC-NFS to the *pcnfsd* computer which returns the corresponding user and group IDs. These IDs are then used by all NFS requests.

PC-NFS also allows printer output to be redirected from the PC to the UNIX computer. Here, print requests in the PC are stored as files in a spool area mounted over NFS. To start the printing, a print request is sent to *pcnfsd* which hands the file over to the UNIX spool system.

On some systems, *pcnfsd* is delivered with NFS, but it is also provided in source code with PC-NFS and must in the latter case be ported to the UNIX computer used as NFS server.

## spray and sprayd

The program *spray* and the corresponding server *sprayd*, like the program *ping*, are used to test the functional integrity of a computer; in addition to ICMP, they also use RPC requests. *spray* sends a number of consecutive RPC requests to the *sprayd* computer, without waiting for acknowledgements. Normally, a total of 100000 bytes is transmitted. In addition, the actual number of RPC requests received and the duration of the whole process in the server are queried. The client may use these numbers to determine how many RPC requests were lost, and the number of packets and bytes per second that the server computer is capable of processing.

Using the $-i$ option, the same test procedure may be executed using ICMP echo requests. Here, the throughput is determined in the send and the receive direction. Other *spray* options relate to the number of packets to be sent and their size and length.

## fsirand

*fsirand* is used to preset the generation numbers in the inodes and the file system ID of an NFS server file system to random numbers. In BSD systems, *fsirand* should be executed on every file system before the system is brought into operation as NFS server and in every newly installed file system which is to be exported over NFS.

## Quotas in the operation of NFS

Quotas are features of BSD systems which allow the network administrator to limit the disk space assigned to individual user IDs. Thus, every file system contains a so-called quota file in its root directory with entries giving the maximum number of file blocks assignable to specific user IDs. Commands are available which permit the user and the network administrator, respectively, to interrogate and modify the contents of the quota file.

Quotas are only defined in the Berkeley fast-file system. Since the NFS server process uses the file system interface in the same way as any other process, it is also subject to the file access restrictions determined by quotas for a specific user ID.

An RPC protocol called *remote quota* (RQUOTA) with program number 100011 and server *rquotad* is used to interrogate the quotas in file systems on NFS server computers. The RPC procedures contained in it supply the same information as a local *quotactl* system call. The RQUOTA service is needed because the local super-user login name does not have access to the quota file over NFS (see *nobody* login name), and furthermore access to the quota information of currently unmounted file systems is impossible.

# NFS start-up, operation and management

Installation and start-up of NFS varies from manufacturer to manufacturer; thus, it is difficult to give a generally valid specific example. There are however basic considerations and steps which must be taken into account and executed, respectively.

We have already covered most aspects in the previous chapters, but at the end of this section we shall bring together the main points, by way of a checklist for the reader.

## Organizational viewpoint

The operation of a network and the networking of computers with NFS is not a trivial matter and requires a certain preparation and regular attention from a trained person, the network administrator, during the operation.

Neglect of management, particularly in the YP subsystem area, soon leads to disorganization of the files, which requires some effort to sort out. Thus, it is most important for the organization as a whole that there should be *one* person who is responsible for the management of the whole network and whose duties include the allocation of user IDs, which is one of the main 'security' problems.

Another crucial factor in NFS performance is the NFS server. To achieve optimal throughput over NFS, the server's operating system should be perfectly tuned and matched with the appropriate hardware, especially hard disk, disk controller and Ethernet controller, to accommodate the projected load. Otherwise, too much potential bandwidth is sacrificed to the weakest member in the chain, whichever hardware or software component this may be.

## Diagnosis

As a rule, on smaller networks, it is possible to get away with the commands and diagnostic programs supplied with the TCP/IP and NFS software. In larger networks in which perfect operation also has financial and organizational dimensions, it is advisable to use an Ethernet monitor to monitor the network in respect of transmission quality and loading, since errors or bottlenecks are mostly compensated for by the software and thus may remain unnoticed for long periods. However, in the long term, they may lead to a perceptible deterioration in the overall operation.

On larger scale networks, network management systems which are capable of constantly monitoring the operation of the network and the participating systems should be employed. In addition to the detection of errors on the transmission medium by a network monitor, network management systems are able to detect degradations of server performance and shifts of work load within the network, for example, from one NFS server to another.

## Checklist for starting up the network

The first step is to start up the TCP/IP subsystem:

- Installation of the Ethernet hardware including correct installation of switches and bridges and connection to the coaxial cable.
- Choice of a host name for every computer.
- Choice of a network ID.
- Choice of a host ID for every computer.
- Installation of the TCP/IP software.
- Addition of */etc/hosts* (and under certain circumstances of */etc/hosts.equiv*) to all computers.
- Start-up of the TCP/IP system on all computers.
- Test.

Then follows the installation of NFS:

- Choice of a domain name.
- Installation of the NFS software.
- Choice and installation of the master server for the YP maps.
- Choice and installation of the slave server and activation of periodic updates.
- Installation of the master files for the YP maps, with information such as host names, etc., from the other (possibly operational) computers.
- Adjustment of user and group IDs on all computers in the network and elimination of overlaps.
- Alteration of owner entries of all files to the newly established user IDs.
- Modification of */etc/passwd* and */etc/group* on the slave computers to permit access to all user IDs over YP.
- Installation of the entries in */etc/exports* in the individual computers.
- Installation of the entries in */etc/fstab* in the individual computers.

- Activation of *portmap*.
- Activation of the YP subsystem (*ypserv, ypbind*) on all computers.
- Activation of the NFS subsystem (*nfsd, biod, mountd,* etc.) on all computers.
- Test YP and NFS.
- If necessary, adjustment of the system resources and tables to the additional requirements of NFS and/or TCP/IP (for example, increase in the size of some system tables, buffer areas, etc.).

# Remote file system organization

NFS may be used to establish a variety of client/server relationships between systems. The two most prominent reasons for using NFS are to facilitate systems management and to decrease the cost of computer equipment by resource sharing. In real-world terms, this means that the organization of remote file systems accessed through NFS comes in three main flavours:

(1) Centralized, where one or more servers provide disk storage for the entire system population, which is either diskless or has only limited storage capacity. This has advantages in both systems management (for example, central back-up/restore) and resource sharing.

(2) Dedicated, where a particular server contains a particular file tree, for example, a source code server or a server on which all Login directories are located. The latter is particularly useful, in that it is possible to create a single system view where a user may login to every system in the network and may always access his Login directory under the same path name.

(3) Meshed, where systems mount a particular file tree on another system for some purpose but are otherwise entirely self-contained.

Clearly, remote mounts also have their disadvantages: if, for any reason, the remote system which acts as a server is not active, applications and utilities may cease to operate if they require data or a response from the remote server. With many active remote mounts, the chance of a server failing increases accordingly.

If you have mounted a file system on a colleague's workstation and this person likes to switch off his workstation when leaving the office, you may experience all kinds of disturbances. One simple example of an otherwise harmless utility which will cause a problem in a situation of this type is the UNIX command *df*, which, when executed, gets stuck while it waits for a response from each server which is mounted. Some systems like to display the amount of free disk space during the login procedure; if a server is not active, you will not be able to log into the system until the server becomes active again.

This simple example makes it clear that care must be taken when designing an NFS network. Clearly, servers should be systems which are up most of the time; this can be easily achieved for centralized or dedicated servers. If access to a file system is only sporadically required, the use of an automounter may be a good idea, as it automatically adjusts the number of active remote mounts to the required minimum.

# 11

# Programmer interfaces

- Socket interface
- TLI and XTI
- RPC/XDR programming

This chapter describes the interfaces to TCP/IP and RPC/XDR which enable the UNIX programmer to develop his own distributed applications.

# Socket interface

## Background

For the first time in UNIX systems, 4.2BSD introduced a group of programmer interfaces specifically designed for communication between processes, the so-called *socket interface* (named after the first system call of the group). At that time, sockets were revolutionary, since they were constructed as generic communication interfaces: in addition to TCP and UDP, they may also be used for local interprocess communication in the so-called *UNIX domain*. Moreover, they allow access at the IP level.

The socket interfaces are not uncontroversial. Initially, they served only two different communication domains: Internet and UNIX. In 4.3BSD, the *Xerox Network System* (XNS) protocols were added. Many applications using the socket interfaces were developed and today they are found in almost all TCP/IP implementations. Important technologies such as the X window system from MIT, NFS from Sun Microsystems and DCE from OSF use sockets and TCP/IP.

While socket interfaces have not been standardized by any institution, they are however a *de facto* industry standard. This is largely because they are easy to understand and are accommodated completely harmoniously in the UNIX environment. An extended socket interface to support the ISO protocols is planned for release in 4.4BSD.

## System calls

One of the main design criterion for socket interfaces was their seamless integration into existing UNIX system interfaces. We may add that this criterion was fulfilled without giving up any of the flexibility with which very different network architectures are served. The symmetry of the interfaces used in server and client programs is initially striking. Except for limited compulsory differences, the same sequence of system calls is executed on connection set-up by the client and on connection acceptance by the server (see Table 11.1).

One particular advantage of the integration of TCP/IP in UNIX is the fact that TCP, like UNIX files, is not record but stream oriented. Since the standard system calls *read* and *write* are sufficient for almost all input and output under TCP, existing programs may be run in a networked environment without problems (see *rsh*).

**Table 11.1**   Socket interfaces in client or server programs.

| Phase | Active | Passive |
|---|---|---|
| Open end point | *socket* | |
| Designate end point | *bind* | |
| Connection set-up (TCP) | *connect* | *listen* |
| | | *accept* |
| Send data | *write, send* | |
| | *sendto, sendmsg* | |
| Receive data | *read, recv* | |
| | *recvfrom, recvmsg* | |
| Close connection (TCP) | *shutdown* | |
| Shut down end point | *close* | |
| Miscellaneous | *getpeername, getsockname* | |
| | *getsockopt, setsockopt* | |
| Accept input from multiple sources | *select* | |

Although UDP-based communication end points may be operated with standard system calls, they usually necessitate additional transmission-reliability related expenses. Thus, as a rule, UDP is only used in areas, such as transaction-oriented processing, where in most cases there is a separate application-specific interface above the socket interface (for example, RPC).

Although the BSD system call *select()* is not a special interface for data communications, it is often used in distributed applications. It permits simultaneous waiting for data from several data sources.

In BSD-based systems, sockets are a component of the standard C library */lib/libc.a*. In many implementations in System V.3 or earlier, the socket interfaces are not true system calls, but are emulated by library routines and are contained in other libraries such as */usr/lib/libsocket.a* or */usr/lib/libinet.a* which must be explicitly specified when linking programs. The same is true of the additional library routines described later in the chapter.

## Header files and address structures

In order to use sockets, programs must include several header files. As shown in Figure 11.1, one begins with *sys/socket.h* and *netinet/in.h* which contain the most important data structures and parameters for use with sockets and TCP/IP. Since both these files use special type declarations, the file *sys/types.h* must be included beforehand.

Library routines are very often used to read information from the configuration files from */etc* or YP maps. These routines return pointers

```
#include <sys/types.h>  /* needed by others */
#include <sys/socket.h> /* socket types and flags */
#include <netinet/in.h> /* internet declarations */

#include <netdb.h>      /* get...by...  services */
```

**Figure 11.1** Typical header files for a socket program.

to structures which are defined in *netdb.h*.

BSD systems support several different protocol families including TCP/IP, UNIX and XNS. The socket system calls are designed to work with different address structures. The first entry of every address structure is a field which specifies the address type. The example in Figure 11.2 shows the Internet-specific structure *struct_sockaddr_in*. The TCP/IP programmer enters the value of AF_INET in the *sin_family* field. The fields *sin_port* and *sin_addr* contain the port number and the Internet address, given in the network format which defines the byte sequence in binary integers. There are also corresponding routines for conversion from local into network format, which we shall not go into.

For historical reasons, the address itself *sin_addr* is a structure, although there would be room for it in an *unsigned long*. The complete *sock_addr_in* structure is padded to 16 bytes in the *sin_zero* field.

```
/*
 * Internet address (a structure for historical reasons)
 */
struct in_addr { u_long s_addr; };

/*
 * Socket address, internet style.
 */
struct sockaddr_in {
    short   sin_family;
    u_short sin_port;
    struct  in_addr sin_addr;
    char    sin_zero[8];
};
```

**Figure 11.2** Declaration of the Internet address.

**Table 11.2**   Other frequently used system and library calls.

| | | | |
|---|---|---|---|
| bcopy | bcmp | bzero | |
| htonl | htons | ntohl | ntohs |
| gethostname | sethostname | | |
| gethostent | gethostbyname | gethostbyaddr | |
| getnetent | getnetbyname | getnetbyaddr | |
| getservent | getservbyname | getservbyport | |
| getprotoent | getprotobyname | getprotobynumber | |
| inet_addr | inet_network | inet_ntoa | |
| inet_makeaddr | inet_lnaof | inet_netof | |
| rcmd | rresvport | ruserok | rexec |
| res_mkquery | res_send | res_init | |
| dn_comp | dn_expand | | |

## Other library routines

In addition to the socket interfaces, there are a number of other library routines without which socket programming would be inconceivable. These routines (see Table 11.2) are used in so many programs that they have practically become a component part of the socket interface. The most important routines include copying, comparison and deletion of data regions (*bcopy*, *bcmp*, *bzero*). Equally crucial are the routines to convert *shorts* and *longs* from network into host format, and vice versa (*ntohs*, *ntohl*, *htons*, *htonl*). *gethostname* is used in many programs to determine the name of one's own computer. The *get* routines read and fetch entries in the configuration files from /etc or YP maps; the *inet_* routines re-organize and convert Internet addresses. *rcmd* and *rexec* are interfaces to the *rshd* and *rexecd* servers. The *res_* and *dn_* routines are interfaces for the DNS resolver.

# TLI and XTI

The Transport Level Interface (TLI) was first supplied with System V Release 3 and STREAMS. It follows the *ISO transport service definition* specified in IS 8072-1986 (connection oriented) and IS 8072/Add.1-1986 (connectionless) very closely. XTI ('X/Open transport interface') denotes an improved form developed by X/Open in which the interfaces to TLI are scarcely altered.

**Table 11.3**   Overview of XTI/TLI library interfaces.

| | | |
|---|---|---|
| t_accept | t_alloc | t_bind |
| t_close | t_connect | t_error |
| t_free | t_getinfo | t_getstate |
| t_listen | t_look | t_open |
| t_optmgmt | t_rcv | t_rcvconnect |
| t_rcvdis | t_rcvrel | t_rcvudata |
| t_rcvuderr | t_snd | t_snddis |
| t_sndrel | t_sndudata | t_sync |
| t_unbind | | |

TLI/XTI was conceived as a generic interface to arbitrary transport protocols and as such is also able to serve TCP/IP.

Many of the names of the TLI/XTI interfaces (see Table 11.3) are very similar to those of the socket interfaces. On some systems, not all functions of TCP/IP are obtainable both in the socket interfaces and over TLI/XTI. A further disadvantage of TLI/XTI is that there are no routines (such as *gethostbyname()*) for address allocation or name conversion.

TLI has a synchronous and an asynchronous mode of operation. The application may either wait for an event to occur or be informed of an event by a signal (in which case it must find out the reason for the event). Only a synchronous interface is specified for XTI.

In STREAMS-based TLI/XTI implementations, part of the interface operation is handled within the UNIX system kernel in a special STREAMS module called *timod*, which must be pushed on to the current protocol stack before TLI/XTI is used. The interface between the protocol modules and *timod* is officially called the Transport Provider Interface (TPI). Any protocol stacks may be used below this interface.

Another STREAMS module called *tirdwr* is required for *read* and *write* operations over network connections. This module converts the read and write requests into STREAMS protocol elements.

# RPC/XDR programming

## Libraries

UNIX systems with NFS usually contain a program interface for C to RPC and XDR. A programmer may use these C subroutines to implement

Table **11.4**   Overview of the XDR library interfaces.

| | | |
|---|---|---|
| xdr_array | xdr_bool | xdr_bytes |
| xdr_destroy | xdr_double | xdr_enum |
| xdr_float | xdr_getpos | xdr_inline |
| xdr_int | xdr_long | xdr_opaque |
| xdr_reference | xdr_setpos | xdr_short |
| xdr_string | xdr_u_int | xdr_u_long |
| xdr_u_short | xdr_union | xdr_void |
| xdr_wrapstring | xdrmem_create | xdrrec_create |
| xdrrec_endofrecord | xdrrec_eof | xdrrec_skiprecord |
| xdrstdio_create | | |

his own RPC services.

On systems of the BSD line, the RPC/XDR routines are mostly already contained in the standard C library */lib/libc.a*; thus, the linking of RPC programs does not require further entries.   Under System V, the RPC/XDR libraries are mostly integrated separately, being found under names such as */usr/lib/librpc.a*.  Since the RPC/XDR routines usually require interfaces to TCP/IP and the socket interface, a network interface library must also be given (for example, */usr/lib/libinet.a* or */usr/lib/libsocket.a*).

## XDR routines

Before we consider a sample program, a brief overview of the routines available in the libraries and of their structure will be given.

The routines in the XDR library (see Table 11.4) handle the basic C components and additional internal functions.

## RPC routines

The RPC routines listed in Table 11.5 provide the user with an interface consisting of several layers of varying complexity. Thus, they allow the user to have a variably strong impact, but require differing depths of knowledge of the functional description of RPC and XDR.

The topmost layer is designed for the application programmer who only generates programs with limited functionality. Complex data structures and access rights are not handled. This layer includes the routines *registerrpc()*, *callrpc()* and *svc_run()*. The UDP transport protocol is used as standard. This layer makes use of the level below, where it is possible to access interface parameters directly, to construct RPC messages (for example, for authentication) and to select the transport protocol used.

**Table 11.5**  Overview of the RPC library interfaces.

| | | |
|---|---|---|
| registerrpc | callrpc | svc_run |
| clnt_broadcast | clnt_call | clnt_destroy |
| clnt_freeres | clnt_geterr | |
| clnt_pcreateerror | | |
| clnt_perrno | clnt_perror | clnt_sperrno |
| clnt_sperror | clntraw_create | clnttcp_create |
| clntudp_create | | |
| svc_destroy | svc_freeargs | svc_getargs |
| svc_getcaller | svc_getreq | svc_register |
| svc_sendreply | svc_unregister | |
| svcerr_auth | svcerr_decode | svcerr_noproc |
| svcerr_noprog | svcerr_progvers | |
| svcerr_systemerr | | |
| svcerr_weakauth | | |
| svcraw_create | svctcp_create | svcudp_create |
| pmap_getmaps | pmap_getport | pmap_rmtcall |
| pmap_set | pmap_unset | |
| auth_destroy | authnone_create | authunix_create |
| authunix_create_default | | |
| xdr_accepted_reply | xdr_authunix_parms | xdr_callhdr |
| xdr_callmsg | xdr_opaque_auth | xdr_pmap |
| xdr_pmaplist | xdr_rejected_reply | xdr_replymsg |
| xprt_register | xprt_unregister | |

This level includes routines with prefix *clnt_* on the client side and prefix *svc_* on the server side. The topmost and middle layers may be combined in a program.

The underlying basic routines are used by all layers. A programmer will scarcely ever have to access this level himself. The RPC protocol, the port mapper dialogue and several fundamental objects are implemented at this level. The prefix *pmap_* stands for port mapper, *auth_* stands for authentication and routines beginning with *xdr_* implement XDR objects.

## Example of an RPC program

### Client program

We shall use the next example to show how easy it is to develop an RPC program. Our example of an RPC program is called DAYPROG and has

```
/*
 * day.h - Header file for the day service
 */
#define DAYPROG         1000000000
#define DAYVERS         1
#define DAYPROC         1
```

**Figure 11.3**   Parameters of the day service in the *day.h* file.

version number DAYVERS. It consists of a client and a server program, where the server program is executed as a single RPC procedure DAYPROC, which returns the current date as a result. The client program outputs this date to the terminal. The program, version and procedure numbers are specified in the file *day.h* (see Figure 11.3) and are included in both the server and the client.

Program numbers may be freely chosen, although Sun's specifications on reserved program number areas should be observed (see RPC protocol). The file *day.c* (see Figure 11.4) contains the client program.

The routine *callrpc()* carries out all actions required for the internal execution of the RPC request, including opening a communication end point, communication with the port mapper and the server, retransmission in the case of failure and conversion of parameters and results.

## Server

Figure 11.5 shows the definition of an RPC user service consisting of the following steps:

- Specification of a program, version and procedure number.
- Specification of the input parameter type, in our case *void*.
- Specification of the return value type, in our case *int*.
- Transfer of the address of the function *day()* to *registerrpc()*.
- Call to *svc_run*.

*registerrpc()* registers the required procedure, both internally and with the port mapper. In *svc_run*, the server then waits for incoming RPC requests and automatically activates the procedure *day()* after converting the procedure parameters into the local format. The server does not return from *svc_run()*. If it is desired to halt this process, a separate procedure must be defined or the server must be stopped with an external signal.

```
/*
 * day.c - Client program for the day service
 */
#include <stdio.h>
#include <rpc/rpc.h>
#include "day.h"

main(argc, argv)
int argc;
char **argv;
{
  int day;
  /* Check whether computer name entered */
  if (argc < 2) {
      fprintf(stderr, "Call:  day computer name\n");
      exit(1);
    }
  /* Execution of the RPC request */
  if (callrpc(*++argv, DAYPROG, DAYVERS, DAYPROC,
              xdr_void, 0, xdr_int, &day) != 0) {
      fprintf(stderr, "Error in callrpc\n");
      exit(1);
    }
  /* Output of results and termination */
  printf("Today is day %d of the month\n", day);
  exit(0);
}
```

**Figure 11.4**   Client program.

## rpcgen

When defining more complicated protocols with many new data types
(which is often the case), the lower layers of the RPC/XDR library should
be used. The RPC program generator *rpcgen* is a tool to support the
programmer, which automatically generates RPC/XDR programs from a
definition file.

Figure 11.6 again shows the file *day.x* which defines the day service.
By convention *rpcgen* definition files have the suffix *.x*. From the definition
file, the generator generates XDR routines and header files containing
the declarations of DAYPROG, DAYVERS and DAYPROC, as required.
Parameters and results are defined in the XDR language, which was
discussed in Chapter 9.

```
/*
 * dayd.c - Server program for the day service
 */
#include <stdio.h>
#include <rpc/rpc.h>
#include "day.h"

day()
{ long t;
  struct tm *tmp;

  /* Determination of the day number */
  time(&t);
  tmp = localtime(&t);
  return (char *)&tmp→tm_mday;
}

main()
{ /* Registration of the service */
  registerrpc(DAYPROG, DAYVERS, DAYPROC,
              day, xdr_void, xdr_int);
  /* Start of the (infinite) server loop */
  svc_run();
}   /* main */
```

**Figure 11.5**   Server program.

In addition, a server program skeleton and, from NFS Version 4.0, a client program skeleton may be generated. These program skeletons only require the programmer to add code for the actions of the individual RPC procedures and thus save him (at least in part) from having to learn the specifications for RPC or XDR programmer interfaces by heart.

```
/*
 * day.x - Definition of the day service
 */
program DAYPROG {
  version DAYVERS {
    int DAYPROC(void) = 1;
  } = 1;
} = 1000000000;
```

**Figure 11.6**   Definition of the day service using *rpcgen*.

If special functions such as verification of access rights or broadcast are used, some knowledge of the interfaces is required, since the RPC program generator is out of its depth here. It is also very easy to extend the program skeletons produced by the generator in the above respects.

## Summary

Nowadays, only RPC/XDR should be used to create networked applications. The advantages of this approach, over classical programming, for example, using socket interfaces, include the following:

- The RPC concept enables easier and more structured design of protocols.
- The data conversion required in a heterogeneous network is automatic and implicit.
- The higher levels of abstraction of the RPC/XDR interfaces make programs created with them more independent of the underlying network protocols and programmer interfaces.

Until System V Release 4, the RPC mechanism described here was still contained in the (separate) NFS package. It has now been enhanced to use the TLI interface and thus works over every available transport mechanism, not just TCP and UDP. Over the next few years, TCP/IP, NFS and RPC/XDR will be included in the SVID and thus they will become part of the basic configuration of all UNIX systems.

# Glossary

**/etc**   Directory on UNIX systems in which programs for configuration and management are stored.

**ACK**   Acknowledgement.

**administrative domain**   Group of computers which for technical administrative purposes belong together.

**advisory**   Principle of file region locking, where processes only experience the existence of locked regions by first-hand checking.

**alias**   Pseudonym.

**application**   User program which supplies the user with information and/or processes data.

**ARP**   Address Resolution Protocol.

**ARPA**   Advanced Research Project Agency.

**ASN.1**   Abstract Syntax Notation One.

**authentication**   Presentation to the server of some form of proof that the client has authorized access to the service facility or to the information it provides. On UNIX systems, the user and group IDs are used.

*awk*   Programmable UNIX text filter command.

**BBN**   Bolt, Beranek & Newman.

**BCD**   Binary-Coded Decimal.

**BER**   Basic Encoding Rules.

**Berkeley File System**   Optimized and particularly fast file system in BSD systems.

**BIND**   Berkeley Internet Name Domain.

**bitmap**   String of bit values, for example, to represent images.

**block**   Unit of data.

**BOOTP**   Bootstrap protocol.

**broadcast**   A message sent to all the stations in the network.

**BSD**   Berkeley System Distribution.

**cache**  Rapidly accessible buffer area for temporary interim storage of information, sometimes associated with algorithms which use behaviour analysis to predict access to certain areas of data and in certain cases store this data in interim storage beforehand.

**CAE**  Common Application Environment.

**CCITT**  Comité Consultatif International Téléphonqiue et Télégraphique.

**client**  User or customer of a service. Sometimes this also designates a role pattern in the relationship between two co-operating processes, where the client takes the active, requesting role.

**cluster**  Combination of several objects into an outwardly indivisible homogeneous unit.

**CMIP**  Common Management Information Protocol.

**CMIS**  Common Management Information Service definition.

**CMOT**  Common Management Information Service over TCP.

**command**  Program executable by a user.

**communication end point**  Logically, an addressable object from which and to which data may be sent. Physically, a collection of related table entries and data structures which define an input/output point for network access in the operating system.

**congestion window**  Volume of data which may be in transmission at a given time.

**connectathon**  Meeting of NFS developers to enable their implementations to communicate with one another.

**cookie**  Unknown data object which can only be evaluated by its creator.

**CRC**  Cyclic Redundancy Check.

*cron*  UNIX daemon for the time-controlled automatic execution of command procedures.

**CSMA/CD**  Carrier Sense Multiple Access with Collision Detection.

**cut and paste**  Extract data from one place and transfer it to another.

**daemon**  UNIX jargon for a user program which is usually loaded on system start, runs in the background until system termination and executes jobs.

**DARPA**  Defence Advanced Research Project Agency.

**data corruption**  Alteration of data due to external effects.

**datagram**  A self-contained message.

**DCE**  Distributed Computing Environment.

**DEC**  Digital Equipment Corporation.

**DF**  Don't Fragment.

**DIN**  Deutsches Institut für Normung.

**DNS**  Domain Name Service.

**DOD**  Department of Defence.

**driver**  A program module in the operating system which is responsible for service and control of a peripheral building block.

**EGP**  Exterior Gateway Protocol.

**environment variables**  Keyword parameters in the form of ASCII characters which are inherited on UNIX systems when processes are divided.

**EUNET**  European UNIX Network.

**expedited**   Preferentially forwarded information.

**fan-out unit**   Interface multiplexer on LAN networks.

**file system**   This is normally a collection of data and the corresponding administrative information on a storage medium.   In a certain context, it also refers to the implementation of methods of access to data and administrative information.

**FIN**   Final.

**flag**   Variable with truth value true or false (1 or 0).

**fragment**   Piece of an IP message.

**fragmentation**   Process of fragment generation.

**front end**   Stand-alone computer which executes the data transfer protocols for the host.

**FSS**   File System Switch.

**FTP**   File Transfer Protocol.

**GECOS**   General Electric Computer Operating System.

**GECOS field**   Field in a data record of the file */etc/passwd* on UNIX systems. In the early days of UNIX, this field was reserved for the GECOS operating system. Today, its meaning is unspecified and it is used to hold various information (for example, the name of the user, etc.).

**hash code**   A pointer to a data record, which may be determined using a function of the data or its key.

**HDLC**   High-level Data Link Control.

**host**   Computer on which applications may be executed.

**IAB**   Internet Activities Board.

**ICMP**   Internet Control Message Protocol.

**ID**   Identification.

**identification**   Unambiguous designation, mostly numerical.

**IEEE**   Institute of Electrical and Electronics Engineers.

**IEN**   Internet Engineering Note.

**IMP**   Internet Message Processor.

**inode (index node)**   Catalogue entry for storing file attributes on UNIX file systems.

**IP**   Internet Protocol.

**ISO**   International Standardization Organization.

**KLM**   Kernel Lock Manager.

**LAN**   Local Area Network.

**layer**   Functional unit.

**library**   Collection of program modules in a file.

**link**   Reference to the same physical file by several file names.

**LLC**   Logical Link Control.

**lock**   Locked data area.

**login**   Terminal session.

*login*   UNIX command to open a terminal session.

**Login directory** Directory which becomes the current directory on opening a terminal session.

**loopback** Reflect back.

*ls* UNIX command to list file names.

**LU6.2** Logical Unit 6.2.

**MAC** Media Access Control.

**mailbox** Object in which electronic mail may be stored.

*make* UNIX development tool for configuration management in software projects.

*makefile* Command file for the UNIX development tool *make*.

**mandatory locking** Instruction to the operating system to check for the existence of a locked area on file access by processes.

**master** Privileged instance of an object (for example, a server) which is capable of taking control of the other objects of the same class.

**memory management** This includes, for example, the conversion of virtual program addresses into real storage addresses, access protection on memory pages, etc.

**MF** More Fragments.

**MIB** Management Information Base.

**MIL-STD** Military Standard.

**module** A self-contained part of a program which may be used in specific interfaces.

**MSL** Maximum Segment Lifetime.

**MTU** Maximum Transfer Unit.

**multicast** Message to a group of stations in the network (see also **broadcast**).

**multivendor show** Demonstration by several manufacturers.

**NCP** Network Control Program.

**NCS** Network Computing System.

**Network administrator** Person responsible for the administration of the network and the relevant networked components of the connected systems (may be identical with the network manager).

**NFS** Network File System.

**NIC** Network Information Centre.

**NIS** Network Information Service.

**NLM** Network Lock Manager.

**node** A computer which serves several network connections simultaneously. This may be a host, a gateway, a router or a bridge.

**NVT** Network Virtual Terminal.

**option** Possible setting, functional switch.

**OSF** Open Software Foundation.

**OSI** Open Systems Interconnection.

**paging** Function of memory management, to read in individual program pages from the memory medium and store them in the main memory and vice versa.

**path name** Strings of a name separated by slashes, which denote an object in the file system.

**POSIX**  Portable Operating System Interface on UNIX.

**protocol**  Agreement between two communicating entities regarding the type and format of message exchange between them.

**protocol header**  Area preceding data with information for the partner of a protocol layer participating in the data transmission.

*ps*  UNIX command to list active processes.

**pseudo terminal**  Virtual device in the operating system which communicates with a program instead of a terminal.

**PSH**  Push.

**RARP**  Reverse Address Resolution Protocol.

**regular expression**  Description of a search pattern in text lines.

**result**  The information obtained during the execution of a program, or a returned value.

**REX**  Remote Execution Service.

**RFC**  Request For Comment.

**RFS**  Remote File Sharing.

**RFT**  Request For Technology.

**RIP**  Routing Information Protocol.

**route**  Path through several connected networks.

**RPC**  Remote Procedure Call.

**RR**  Resource Record.

**RST**  Reset.

**RTO**  Retransmission timeout.

**RTT**  Round Trip Time.

**run-time environment**  The attributes and parameters determining the execution of a process (for example, user and group IDs, current directory, run-time variables, etc.).

**script**  File with commands which is processed by a command interpreter.

**segment**  Message block in TCP.

**server**  Partner providing service in the relationship between two co-operating processes.

**slave**  Entity which cannot act independently. The master/slave role pattern should not necessarily be compared with the client/server role pattern (see also **master**).

**sliding window**  In data-transmission protocols, a principle applied to optimize the data throughput, using parallel send and acknowledgement of data units. Here, the available buffer capacity designated by the receiver for the receipt of data is viewed as a window relative to transmitted but unacknowledged data units, which increases or decreases in size in the course of transmission.

**SLIP**  Serial Line IP.

**SMB**  Server Message Block.

**SMTP**  Simple Mail Transfer Protocol.

**SNAP**  Subnetwork Access Protocol.

**SNMP**  Simple Network Management Protocol.

**SQL**  Structured Query Language.

**SRI**  Stanford Research Institute.

**SRTT**  Smoothed Round Trip Time.

*stderr*  Standard error channel for error messages in UNIX processes.

*stdin*  Standard input channel in UNIX processes.

*stdout*  Standard output channel in UNIX processes.

**subsystem**  Self-contained system which may be installed and activated as a whole.

**SVID**  System V Interface Definition.

**SYN**  Synchronize.

**System V**  UNIX variant developed and sold by AT&T, the continuing development of which takes the form of ongoing releases. The current version is System V Release 4, released in December 1989.

**TCP**  Transmission Control Protocol.

**terminal identifier**  Terminal type identifier used for the *termcap* or *terminfo* control character database.

**test suite**  A collection of programs to check the functional capability of a system.

**TFTP**  Trivial File Transfer Protocol.

**three-way handshake**  Three-way message exchange on connection set-up.

**time sharing**  Technique for multiple use of a computer installation, where the operating system allocates each user part of the computing facility over a time slice.

**timer**  Time-controlled alarm function.

**TLI**  Transport Level Interface.

**TPI**  Transport Provider Interface.

**trailer**  A protocol header stored after the data.

**TTL**  Time To Live.

**UCLA**  University of California, Los Angeles.

**UCSB**  University of California, Santa Barbara.

**UDP**  User Datagram Protocol.

**URG**  Urgent.

**user program**  Program which runs not in the privileged part of the operating system but outside the operating system kernel.

**UUCP**  UNIX-to-UNIX copy.

**validation**  Check that the functionality conforms with the specification.

**VFS**  Virtual File System.

**WYSIWYG**  What You See Is What You Get.

**XDR**  External Data Representation.

**XNS**  Xerox Network System.

**XPG**  X/Open Portability Guide.

**XTI**  X/Open Transport Interface.

**YP**  Yellow Pages.

# Contact addresses

Contact address of the IAB:

Jon Postel
Deputy Internet Architect
USC Information Sciences Institute
4676 Admiralty Way
Marina del Rey
CA 90292-6695
USA
1-213-822-1511
Email: Postel@ISI.EDU

Official Internet numbers are issued by:

Joyce K. Reynolds
Internet Assigned Numbers Authority
USC Information Sciences Institute
4676 Admiralty Way
Marina del Rey
CA 90292-6695
USA
1-213-822-1511
Email: JKRey@ISI.EDU

Address of the publisher of RFCs:

Jon Postel
RFC Editor
USC Information Sciences Institute
4676 Admiralty Way
Marina del Rey
CA 90292-6695
USA
1-213-822-1511
Email: Postel@ISI.EDU

Address of the NIC for information about
RFCs:

SRI International
DDN Network Information Centre
333 Ravenswood Avenue
Menlo Park
CA 94025
USA
1-800-235-3155, 1-415-859-3695
Email:NIC@SRI-NIC.ARPA

# Bibliography

Callaghan B. and Lyon T. (1989). *The Automounter Proceedings of the 1989 Winter USENIX Technical Conf.*, San Diego

Cerf V. (1988). *IAB Recommendations for the Development of Internet Network Management Standards.* RFC 1052

Croft B. and Gilmore J. (1985). *Bootstrap Protocol (BOOTP).* RFC 951

Davin J. *et al.* (1990). *Simple Network Management Protocol (SNMP).* RFC 1157

DEC, Intel and Xerox (1982). *The Ethernet – A Local Area Network Data Link Layer and Physical Layer Specifications*

Deering S. (1988). *Host Extensions for IP Multicasting.* RFC 1054

DOD (1983a). *DOD, Military Standard Internet Protocol.* MIL-STD 1777

DOD (1983b). *DOD, Military Standard Transmission Control Protocol.* MIL-STD 1778

Finlayson R. (1984). *Ross Bootstrap Loading Using TFTP.* RFC 906

Finlayson R. *et al.* (1984). *A Reverse Address Resolution Protocol.* RFC 903

Hedrick C. (1988). *Routing Information Protocol.* RFC 1058

Hornig C. (1984). *A Standard for the Transmission of IP Datagrams over Ethernet Networks.* RFC 894

IEEE (1983, 1984, 1985, 1986). *Standard IEEE 802 Local Area Networks.* IEEE Publication Service

IEEE (1985). *IEEE Standard for Binary Floating-point Arithmetic.* ANSI/IEEE Standard 754-1985

ISO (1987a). *Information Processing systems – Open Systems Interconnection – Specification of Abstract Syntax Notation One (ASN.1).* International Standard 8824

ISO (1987b). *Information Processing Systems – Open Systems Interconnection – Specification of Basic Encoding Rules for Abstract Syntax Notation One (ASN.1).* International Standard 8825

ISO/IEC 9595. *Information Processing Systems – Open Systems Interconnection – Management Information Service Definition*

ISO/IEC 9596. *Information Processing Systems – Open Systems Interconnection – Management Information Protocol Definition*

Jacobson V. (1990). *TCP/IP Headers for Low-speed Serial Links.* RFC 1144

Juszczak C. (1989). Improving the Performance and Correctness of an NFS Server. In *Proc. 1989 Winter USENIX Technical Conf.*, San Diego

Kirton P. (1984). *EGP Gateway under Berkeley UNIX 4.2.* RFC 911

Korb J. (1983). *A Standard for the Transmission of IP Datagrams over Public Data Networks.* RFC 877

221

Leffler J.S. and Karels M.J. (1984). *Trailer Encapsulations.* RFC 893

McCloghrie K. and Rose M.T. (1990a). *Structure and Identification of Management Information for TCP/IP-based Internets.* RFC 1155

McCloghrie K. and Rose M.T. (1990b). *Management Information Base for Network Management of TCP/IP-based Internets.* RFC 1156

Miller S.P. *et al.* (1987). *Kerberos Authentication and Authorization System. Project Athena Technical Plan Section E.2.1*

Mills D.L. (1983). *DCN Local Network Protocols.* RFC 891

Mills D.L. (1984). *Exterior Gateway Protocol Formal Specification.* RFC 904

Mockapetris P. (1987a). *Domain Names – Concepts and Facilities.* RFC 1034

Mockapetris P. (1987b). *Domain Names – Implementation and Specification.* RFC 1035

Mogul J. and Postel J. (1985). *Internet Standard Subnetting Procedure.* RFC 950

Mogul J. *et al.* (1988). *IP MTU Discovery Options.* RFC 1063

OSI (1984). *Information Processing Systems – Open Systems Interconnection: Basic Reference Model.* International Standardization Organization and International Electrotechnical Committee Standard 7498

Plummer D.C. (1982). *An Ethernet Address Resolution Protocol.* RFC 826

Postel J. (1980). *User Datagram Protocol.* RFC 768

Postel J. (1981a). *Internet Protocol.* RFC 791

Postel J. (1981b). *Internet Control Message Protocol.* RFC 792

Postel J. (1981c). *Transmission Control Protocol.* RFC 793

Postel J. (1982). *Simple Mail Transfer Protocol.* RFC 821

Postel J. and Reynolds J. (1983). *TELNET Protocol Specification.* RFC 854

Postel J. and Reynolds J. (1985). *File Transfer Protocol (FTP).* RFC 959

Postel J. and Reynolds J. (1987). *Assigned Numbers.* RFC 1010

Postel J. and Reynolds J. (1988). *A Standard for the Transmission of IP Datagrams over IEEE 802 Networks.* RFC 1042

Romkey J. (1988). *A Non-standard for Transmission of IP Datagrams over Serial Lines: SLIP.* RFC 1055

Rosen E.C. (1982). *BBN Exterior Gateway Protocol (EGP).* RFC 827

St. Johns M. (1988). *Draft Revised IP Security Option.* RFC 1038

Sämonson L.J. and Rosen E.C. (1984). *'STUB' Exterior Gateway Protocol.* RFC 888

Schneider H.J., ed. (1983). *Lexikon der Informatik und Datenbearbeitung.* Vienna: Oldenbourg

Sollins K.R. (1981). *The TFTP Protocol (Revision 2).* RFC 783

Stahl M. (1987). *Domain Administrators Guide.* RFC 1032

Sun Microsystems (1987). *XDR: External Data Representation Standard.* RFC 1014

Sun Microsystems (1988). *RPC: Remote Procedure Call Specification.* RFC 1050

Sun Microsystems (1989). *NFS: Network File System Protocol Specification.* RFC 1094

Warrier U. and Besaw L. (1989). *Common Management Information Services and Protocol over TCP/IP (CMOT).* RFC 1095

# Index

$HOME/.rhosts  70
/etc  81
  /exports  171, 172
  /gated.cf  103
  /gateways  103
  /group
    group.byname and
      group.bygid  185
    YP maps substitution  187
  /hosts  81
    localhost and loopback  80
    map  154
  /hosts.equiv  70
    as prerequisite for rsh  74
  /inetd.cf  94
  /netgroup  172
  /networks  81
    map  154
  /passwd  152
    format for makedbm  183
    map  154
    super-user name  165
    YP maps substitution  187
  /protocols  82
    map  154
  /services  82
  configuration files  81
  differences in implementations  158

Abstract Syntax Notation 1  109
access modes on the NFS server  162
ACK  33
acknowledgement delay  41
addresses
  at the IP level  23
  DNS database  106

addresses (continued)
  enquiry with ypwhich  190
  extension via rcp  75
  for broadcast under BSD  91
  for Ethernet  48
  in DNS, storage  106
  Internet  23
    types  24
  modification by arp  91
  multi-homing  25
  of computers in the network  81
  of the network layer  50
  port numbers  23
  source and destination
    in the IP protocol header  23
    in the TCP protocol header  31
    in the UDP protocol header  43
  structure in sockets  203
  subnetwork  23
  transport protocol  23
administration
  of the ARP table  91
  of TCP/IP  79
administrative domain for NIS  181
alignment of data structures  131
allocation of port numbers  132
alternatives to NFS  117
Andrew File System  120
application layer of the OSI reference
    model  8
architecture
  comparison of OSI and TCP/IP  14
  OSI  6
  TCP/IP  13
arp  91

223

$ 20